D0861872

The Visual Dictionary
of Graphic Design

An AVA Book
Published by AVA Publishing SA
Rue des Fontenailles 16
Case Postale
1000 Lausanne 6
Switzerland
Tel: +41 786 005 109
Email: enquiries@avabooks.ch

Distributed by Thames & Hudson (ex-North America)
181a High Holborn
London WC1V 7QX
United Kingdom
Tel: +44 20 7845 5000
Fax: +44 20 7845 5055
Email: sales@thameshudson.co.uk
www.thamesandhudson.com

Distributed in the USA & Canada by
Watson-Guptill Publications
770 Broadway
New York, New York 10003
USA
Fax: 1-646-654-5487
Email: info@watsonguptill.com
www.watsonguptill.com

English Language Support Office
AVA Publishing (UK) Ltd.
Tel: +44 1903 204 455
Email: enquiries@avabooks.co.uk

ISBN 2-940373-43-4 and 978-2-940373-43-7

10 9 8 7 6 5 4 3 2 1

Design by Gavin Ambrose
www.gavinambrose.co.uk

Production by AVA Book Production
Pte. Ltd., Singapore
Tel: +65 6334 8173
Fax: +65 6259 9830
Email: production@avabooks.com.sg

The Visual Dictionary of Graphic Design

How to get the most out of this book

This book is an easy-to-use reference to the key terms used in graphic design. Each entry comprises a brief textual definition along with an illustration or visual example of the point under discussion. Supplementary contextual information is also included.

Key areas addressed in this book are those terms commonly used in reference to typography, layout, colour, format, image and artistic movements.

Entries are presented in alphabetical order to provide an easy reference system.

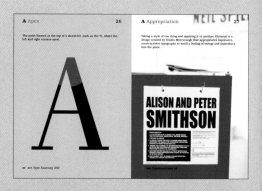

M Median · 160

A method of reducing the values of an image to remove detail without causing pixelation.

☞ see Filters 100

M Metallic · 161

A highly reflective ink or foil with metallic characteristics. Metallic inks are special printing inks, which are outside of the standard gamut of the CMYK or Hexachrome colour spaces. These colours can also be applied to a design through the use of a foil stamp. Pictured is a brochure by SEA Design that features text produced with a metallic foil.

☞ see CMYK 54, Gamut 113

Each page contains a single entry and, where appropriate, a printers' hand symbol ☞ provides page references to other related and relevant entries.

A timeline of graphic design helps to provide historical context for selected key moments in the discipline's development.

Welcome to *The Visual Dictionary of Graphic Design*, a book that provides textual definitions and visual explanations for some of the more common terms found in the key areas of graphic design and pertinent entries from the wider world of graphic arts.

This volume aims to provide a clear understanding of the many terms that are often misused or confused such as *italics* and *obliques*, or the difference between an *overprint*, a *surprint* and a *reverse out*. As you might expect, *The Visual Dictionary of Graphic Design* provides visual explanations, and many of these are examples of commercial work, produced by leading contemporary design studios, to illustrate the correct usage of typographical elements such as the *ellipsis*, the rules for the handling of problems such as *widows, orphans & the hypho* and the correct usage of *numerals* to produce accurate text.

This French poster (far left) uses the text *accents*.

A *vernacular* type style is used by Studio Myerscough for this piece of packaging (left).

Graphic design communicates through a range of visual devices including *montages*, *collages*, *metaphors*, *rhetoric* and *juxtapositions*, all of which, and more, are explained and illustrated.

A clear understanding of the key terms used in graphic design will help you to better articulate and formalise your ideas and ensure accuracy in the transfer of those ideas to others.

This war poster (facing page, far left) features *rhetoric*, the art of persuasion.

This spread (facing page, left) created by Frost Design features a simple text *hierarchy*.

Pictured right, primary colours and shapes were defining features of the *Bauhaus* school.

This poster (right), from typography magazine *Fuse*, features a distorted, *filter*-inspired *typeface* by Brett Wickens.

This poster design (far right) by Peter and Paul features typography that has been *reversed out*.

This (facing page) *slab serif* capital letter was created by Vasava Artworks.

Graphic design is a discipline that continues to evolve. The timeline (page 274) shows how changes in technology have dramatically affected communications in the past, and how technological advancement continues to do so. Coupled with this is the ever changing taste and preference of society, which gives rise to numerous schools of thought about how information should be presented. In the twentieth century, for example, the rise of modernism embraced technological advances and adopted cleaner, less adorned forms, and in doing so rejected the decorative nature of design in Victorian times. However, with time, this too changed and postmodernism saw a move away from industrial nature as designers once again embraced more elaborate and softer visual concepts.

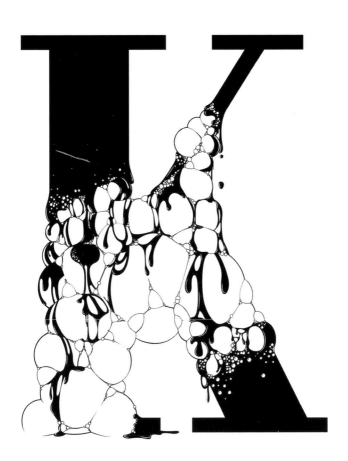

This spread (left) was created by Faydherbe / De Vringer and features a *passe partout*.

Sagmeister Inc. created these designs (below), which feature *mark making*.

ANNI KUAN

HAPPILY INVITES YOU TO THE FASHION COTERIE TO PREVIEW THE FALL AND WINTER 2003 COLLECTION

Pictured above is the *First Things First* manifesto. Written in 1964 by designer Ken Garland it was presented as a backlash against consumer society. The manifesto was signed by over 400 designers and helped place graphic design, which was at that time a relatively young discipline, in a wider social context.

Design professionals draw inspiration from innumerable sources such as their urban environment or by cross referencing elements of contemporary life with those of bygone days, and delving back into the rich tradition of the arts as a means of visual stimulation. Inspiration is key to the generation of exciting design ideas. It is with this in mind that we hope that this book will also serve as a source of ideas to inspire your creativity.

Contents

The Dictionary

The two measurement systems used in typography.

Absolute measurements

Absolute measurements are easy to understand as they are measurements of fixed values. For example, a millimetre is a precisely defined increment of a centimetre. Equally, both points and picas, the basic typographic measurements, have fixed values. All absolute measurements are expressed in finite terms that cannot be altered.

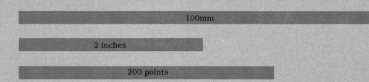

100mm

2 inches

200 points

Relative measurements

In typography, many values, such as character spacing, are directly linked to typesize which means that they are defined by a series of relative (rather than absolute) measurements. The basic building block for typographical characters, the em, is a relative measurement. Type set at 70pt has a 70pt em. Type set at 40pt has a 40pt em.

The em

The em

The em

70pt type gives an em value of 70pts.

Reducing the typesize to 40pt reduces the em value to 40pts.

Further reducing the typesize proportionally reduces the em value.

☞ see Ems & Ens 93

An American art movement that developed in New York City following the Second World War, and featured forms not found in the natural world as a means of emotional expression. Abstract expressionist works were characterised by large canvases with uniform, unstructured coverings that projected power due to their scale. Leading figures in this movement include Jackson Pollock, Mark Rothko and Clyfford Still.

☞ see Dada 71

A range of diacritical marks and symbols which indicate that the sound of a letter is modified during pronunciation. While accents are not a common feature of English, they are relatively common in other languages such as Spanish, French, German and Slavic languages.

Acute
An accent above a vowel angled upwards to the right, which indicates that it is close or tense, has a high or rising pitch, a long pronunciation, or that the syllable in which the vowel appears is stressed. From the Latin *acutus*, meaning 'sharp'.

Circumflex
Shaped like a pointed hat, a circumflex sits above a vowel to indicate that it has a long sound. From the Latin *circumflexus*, meaning 'bent around'.

Breve
A 'v' shaped symbol that indicates a short sounding of the letter. From the Latin *brevis*, which means 'short'.

Grave
An accent above a vowel angled upwards to the left, which indicates stress or special pronunciation. From the Latin *gravis* meaning 'heavy'.

Umlaut / Diaeresis
Two periods over a vowel, which indicate that the sound changes by assimilating the vowel sound of the following syllable. Typical in Germanic languages. From the German *um*, meaning 'around' or 'alteration', and *laut*, meaning 'sound'. Also called diaeresis.

Tilde
A wavy bar placed above a letter to indicate a more nasal pronunciation, such as the Spanish 'ñ', which has the same sound as the 'ny' in 'canyon'. From the medieval Latin *titulus* meaning 'title'.

☛ see Diacritical Marks 82

Additive primaries   **Subtractive primaries**

The red, green and blue (RGB) colours are the primary constituent parts of white light. These colours are called additive primaries because, when added together, they produce white light. Cyan, magenta and yellow are called the subtractive primaries and are used in the four-colour printing process.

Colour reproduction is based on the same principles as the three-colour vision of the human eye. The eye contains three different types of receptors, each of which are sensitive to one of the primary RGB colours of light. Any two additive primaries will create one of the subtractive primaries (as can be seen where the colours overlap in the diagrams above). Similarly, any two subtractive primaries create an additive primary. This is the principle behind the separation process used to reproduce colour images.

☞ see CMYK 54, RGB 212

The positioning of text in relation to the area or text block within which it is contained. In the horizontal plane text can be right, left or centre aligned, or justified.

This text is range left, ragged right and is characterised by being aligned left, allowing a ragged right edge, and the even, unforced spacing between words.

This text is range right, ragged left and is also characterised by the even spacing between words. The ragged left edge may impede easy reading as this can distract the eye and make it difficult to find the start of a line.

This text is centre aligned and is characterised by being aligned through a central point. The ragged left edge may impede easy reading as this can distract the eye and make it difficult to find the start of a line. Equally, awkward shapes can also be formed by the text block.

This text is justified and extends fully to both sides of the text block or column. This is achieved by varying the word spacing, which may result in ugly spaces and several broken words (when hyphenation is used).

This text is forced justified, which means that even if there is only one word in the last line of the paragraph, it will be justified across the measure (the width of the text column) producing an ugly result, as
s   h   o   w   n   .

☞ see Measure 159

A ligature of the Latin word *et*, meaning 'and'. The name ampersand is a contraction of the Latin phrase 'and per se and', which translates as 'the symbol for and by itself means and'. The earliest usage of the ampersand symbol dates back to the first century AD and it is now found in many languages that use the Latin alphabet.

A comparison between one thing and another, made for the purpose
of explanation or clarification. Often refers to the seemingly impossible
or surreal for extra emphasis. For example, a task that appears
impossible is analogous to obtaining blood from a stone. The success
of an implicit analogy in a design is dependent upon the ability of the
target audience to interpret exactly what the analogy is. Analogies
often use the vernacular language in common usage. Pictured above is
a poster created by Sagmeister Inc. that features a headless chicken.
This is an analogy for making a lot of effort and noise, but yielding
little gain.

☞ see Surrealism 241, Vernacular 265

A term used to describe fonts with bracketed slab-serifs and little stroke weight variation. Confusingly, antique is also used to describe some sans-serif fonts as well.

Bookman

ITC Bookman was created by Edward Benguiat in 1975. This font features a large x-height and moderate stroke contrast for optimal legibility.

Antique Olive

Antique Olive was created by French typographer Roger Excoffon in the 1960s. This font has a large x-height and open letterforms, which make it very readable and ideal for smaller point sizes.

☞ see Serif & Sans Serif 223, Type Classification 260, X-height 269

The point formed at the top of a character, such as the 'A', where the left and right strokes meet.

☞ see Type Anatomy 259

Taking a style of one thing and applying it to another. Pictured is a
design created by Studio Myerscough that appropriates expressive,
constructivist typography to instil a feeling of energy and immediacy
into the piece.

see Constructivism 64

Named after the 1925 Exposition Internationale des Arts Décoratifs et Industriels Modernes, which was held in Paris, Art Deco describes a decorative design style that celebrated the rise of technology and speed via geometric designs, intense colours, and the use of plastic and glass. Forms became streamlined as the principles of aerodynamics became better understood resulting in an elegant style in both architecture and objects.

☞ see Geometric 115

Rooted in romanticism and symbolism, **art nouveau** (the new art)
describes a richly ornamental style of decoration, architecture and
art that developed during 1894–1914. Art nouveau is characterised by
undulating lines, sinuous curves and the depiction of leaves, flowers
and flowing vines and is embodied in the work of protagonists such
as Gustav Klimt, Henri de Toulouse-Lautrec, Antonio Gaudi and
Hector Guimard, who was the architect and designer of the Paris
metro entrances.

Called Jugendstil (in Germany), Sezessionstil (in Austria), and
Modernismo (in Spain), art nouveau rejected historical references
in favour of creating a highly stylised design vocabulary that unified all
arts around man and his life. Architecture was the focus for art nouveau
as it naturally encompasses and integrates every art, but
the style was also used extensively in posters and jewellery design.
The ornate typeface used here is Benguiat.

A LATE NINETEENTH CENTURY DECORATIVE ARTS, FURNITURE AND ARCHITECTURE MOVEMENT THAT SOUGHT TO REVERSE THE DEMISE OF BEAUTY AT THE HANDS OF THE INDUSTRIAL REVOLUTION, AND RE-ESTABLISH THE LINK BETWEEN THE WORKER AND ART THROUGH AN HONESTY IN DESIGN. THIS MOVEMENT IS TYPIFIED BY LEADING PROTAGONISTS SUCH AS WILLIAM MORRIS, DANTE GABRIEL ROSSETTI AND FRANK LLOYD WRIGHT.

THIS FONT IS ITC RENNIE MACKINTOSH, WHICH WAS CREATED BY PHILL GRIMSHAW IN 1996. IT IS BASED ON THE HANDWRITING AND DRAWINGS OF SCOTTISH DESIGNER CHARLES RENNIE MACKINTOSH (1868–1928) WHO CREATED HIGHLY ORIGINAL BUILDINGS, INTERIORS AND FURNITURE WITH QUIRKY FLAIR.

ITC RENNIE MACKINTOSH WAS DESIGNED FOLLOWING RESEARCH AND COLLABORATION BETWEEN THE INTERNATIONAL TYPEFACE CORP. AND THE GLASGOW SCHOOL OF ART. THIS FONT FAMILY IS UNUSUAL AND OFF BEAT, AND A GOOD CHOICE FOR PRODUCT PACKAGING, ADVERTISING, AND GRAPHIC DESIGNS WITH A PERIOD FLAIR.

see Typefaces & Fonts 261

The parts of a letter
that extend above the
X-height (ascender) or
below the baseline
(descender).

Ascender

Descender

x-height

Baseline

☞ see Baseline 34, X-height 269

A grid used for page layout that is the same on both the recto and verso pages. Asymmetric grids typically introduce a bias towards one side of the page, usually the left, as pictured here. The additional margin space can be used for notes and captions.

☞ see Recto & Verso 206, Symmetry 243

An artistic work that pushes the established limits of what is considered acceptable. Avant garde works often have revolutionary, cultural, or political connotations.

This page is set in Avant Garde, a font based on the logo designed for `Avant Garde Magazine' in 1967 by Herb Lubalin and Tom Carnase. The font was redrawn in 1970 to include lower case characters.

☞ see Typefaces & Fonts 261

The imaginary line upon which all upper and most lower case letters are positioned. The baseline is a valuable reference for accurate and consistent text and graphic positioning.

The baseline can also be shifted for accurate placement of superscript and subscript characters. Here, the baseline has been shifted by 5pts.

Baseline shift is used to alter the position of subscripts and superiors so that they sit comfortably with body text[1].

☞   see Subscripts 238, Superiors 239

an art and design school opened in 1919 under the direction of the renowned architect walter gropius. the bauhaus aimed to provide a fresh approach to design following the first world war. bauhaus style is characterised by economic and geometric forms. teaching staff included paul klee, wassily kandinsky and marcel breuer.

this page is set in bayer universal, a geometric font that is typical of the bauhaus style.

in 1923 kandinsky proposed that there was a universal relationship between the three basic shapes and the three primary colours (above). he believed the yellow triangle to be the most active and dynamic through to the passive, cold, blue circle.

☞ see Geometric 115

A plastic or paper loop that is used to enclose the pages of a publication. Bellybands are typically seen on consumer magazines, and often include information about the publication's contents. Typically bellybands are a continuous loop, but can also be a strip of stock that is wrapped around a publication.

☞ see Stock 236

A thin, strong, opaque and lightweight paper that helps reduce
the weight of a publication, so named for its predominant use in
bible production. Also called India paper. Pictured is a spread from
13 Typo-Sünden (13 typographic sins) by Hans Peter Willberg,
which was produced for German typography and design studio Verlag
Hermann Schmidt Mainz and is printed on woodfree white 50gsm
bible paper. The vampires in the image represent the erroneous
use of inch marks instead of quotation marks.

☞ see Buckram 47, GSM 123

Any of several bonding processes using stitches, wire, glue or other media to hold together a publication's pages or sections to form a book, magazine, brochure or other format. The most common binding methods are pictured below.

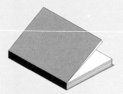

Perfect binding
The backs of sections (signatures) are removed and held together with a flexible adhesive, which also attaches a paper cover to the spine, and the fore edge is trimmed flat. Commonly used for paperback books.

Canadian and half Canadian
A spiral-bound publication with a wraparound cover and an enclosed (Canadian) or an exposed spine (half Canadian).

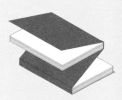

Burst binding
The backs of signatures are slit and held together with a flexible adhesive that is allowed to penetrate rather than being removed (as in perfect binding).

Side stabbing
Wire staples are inserted near the spine from front to back.

Saddle stitch
Signatures are nested and bound with wire stitches applied through the spine along the centrefold.

Z bind
A 'z'-shaped cover that is used to join two separate text blocks, typically with a perfect binding.

☞ **see Canadian Binding 50, Perfect Binding 187, Z Bind 270**

An image constructed of a fixed number of pixels (or dots).
The more frequent and finer the dots are, the sharper and more
detailed is the image produced. Bitmap images can easily be coloured
to create dramatic graphic statements, as the example shown here
demonstrates. Bitmap colouration (of the background or the object)
can be altered without the use of an image-manipulation program.

☞ see Pixel 193

A version of the roman font developed through the 1150–1500 period that is based on the ornate writing style prevalent during the Middle Ages.

Also called Fraktur, Black Letter, Gothic and Old English, these fonts may now appear heavy and difficult to read in large text blocks due to the complexity of their letters and the fact that they seem antiquated and unfamiliar to us.

see Typefaces & Fonts 261

Project1 11/2/06 1:39 pm Page 1

Bleed refers to the information
that extends past the point
where the page will be
trimmed, and allows colour or
images to continue to the very
edge of the cut page.

Trim marks printed around
the image show where the
page will be cut.

The image needs to extend
3mm past the trim marks to
ensure that once the pages are
cut, the image 'bleeds' off
the page.

However, this extra 3mm is
not needed at the binding
edge* as any bleed here will be
lost in the tightness of the
bound book.

* This is the binding edge

SUPER

Mason Super Bold

95

95 Helvetica Black

Poster

Poster Bodoni

Extra

Univers Extra Black

Black

Univers Black

Ultra

GillSans Ultra Bold

Demi

Eurostile Demi

A version of the Roman font with a wider stroke.

Most fonts have a **boldface** version that should be used in preference to the 'fake' bold option that many desktop publishing applications provide. Software applications simply fatten a font rather than giving a true **bold**. A true **bold** will have been crafted to ensure it prints correctly and, more importantly, is in proportion to other weights in the font family.

Boldface is also called medium, semi-bold, black, extra, super or poster, and is represented by a number in Frutiger's Grid.

☞ see Frutiger's Grid 112, Typefaces & Fonts 261

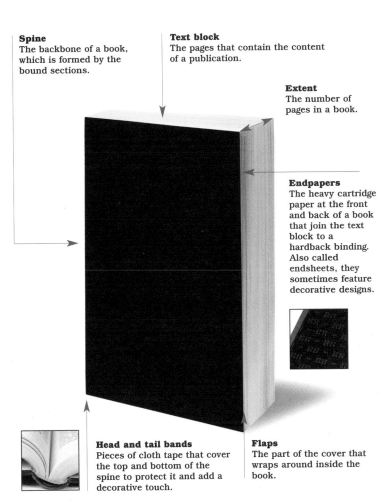

Spine
The backbone of a book, which is formed by the bound sections.

Text block
The pages that contain the content of a publication.

Extent
The number of pages in a book.

Endpapers
The heavy cartridge paper at the front and back of a book that join the text block to a hardback binding. Also called endsheets, they sometimes feature decorative designs.

Head and tail bands
Pieces of cloth tape that cover the top and bottom of the spine to protect it and add a decorative touch.

Flaps
The part of the cover that wraps around inside the book.

☞ see Extent 96, Flaps 101

{ The curly brackets used to enclose any words or text
lines that are to be considered together. Pictured here
is a design by BIS that features braces in Bodoni (the
favourite font of Spanish surrealist artist Salvador Dalí)
to form Dalí's distinctive moustache. }

☞ see Surrealism 241

A symbol, mark, word or phrase that identifies and differentiates a product, service or organisation from its competitors. Brands are created to help us distinguish between similar product offerings through perceptions of quality and value. The brand then becomes a recognisable symbol for a certain level of quality, which aids our buying decision. Brands often craft a 'personality' that represents a set of values which appeal to their target consumers such as foods that are 'healthier', cosmetics that are 'cleaner' or ketchups that are 'saucier' than their competitors.

☞ see Identity, 133

B Broadside

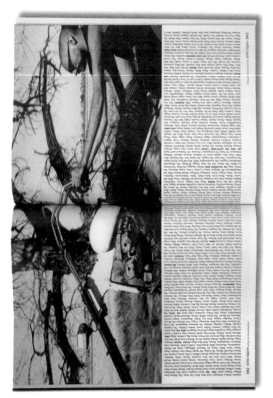

Text that has been rotated 90 degrees to the format of a publication. This is done to make a visual impression or provide a more suitable means of handling text elements within the publication's format such as numeric tables for example. The term derives from maritime warfare when gunboats drew up in battle formation, broadside on, to point the maximum number of guns at enemy shipping. Pictured is a spread from *Zembla* magazine, created by Frost Design studio, which features a long column of broadside text.

see Column 62

A coarse cotton fabric, sized with glue, which is used to stiffen garments and to produce cover stock for book binding. In printing and publishing buckram is used to provide a hard, tactile long-lasting material for case binding. Pictured is a buckram-bound book produced by Studio Thomson that mimics the format of a Moleskine notebook, complete with elastic closure and page-marker band. The book's cover also features a gold-foil block of the title.

☞ see Binding 38, Foil 105

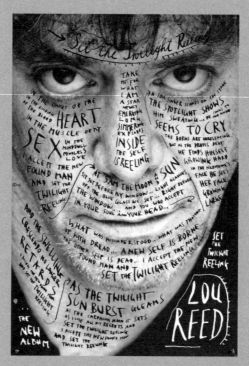

The art of writing by hand, typically with flowing lines and varying stroke thickness, which is achieved by using a chiselled nib or paintbrush. Can also refer to highly stylised and artistic writing styles. Many script fonts try to imitate the calligraphic style, but none result in the same authentic effect as true handwritten letterforms. Pictured is a poster created by Sagmeister Inc., which features handwritten text over an image of musician Lou Reed for an authentic and emotive effect.

☞ see Typefaces & Fonts 261

The thickness of a stock or sheet used in printing. The calliper of a stock has an impact on the feel of a publication, although this does not always imply a precise relationship to the weight of the stock. A thick calliper stock may add a more substantial feel to a publication, while a thin calliper can add a delicate touch. Generally speaking thin calliper stocks tend to have lower weights than thick calliper stocks, but there are papers that have been developed to give added bulk without the weight.

☞ see Stock 237

A book binding method in which the pages are bound with a
metal or plastic spiral with a wraparound cover. The spiral
of a half-Canadian bind is exposed through the cover while that
of a full-Canadian bind is not. Canadian binding effectively combines
the convenience of ring binding (pages can be added/removed) with
the flat, square spine of perfect binding.

☞ see Binding 38

Greyscale information that represents each of the individual colours in the RGB and CYMK systems. Each colour is represented by a separate channel that can be independently altered, replaced or omitted. RGB images have three channels and CMYK images have four.

The unaltered image

Swapping the magenta channel for the yellow one, which produces an effect that is similar to printing the CMYK plates out of sequence

Running the black channel as yellow

Swapping the magenta with cyan

☞ see CMYK 54, RGB 212

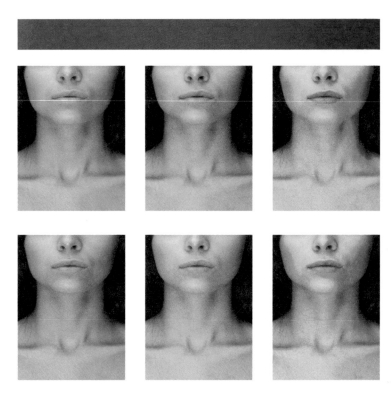

The colour variation of the same tonal brightness from none to pure colour. Chroma or saturation is the strength, purity or amount of grey in relation to the hue.

Pictured here (top row, left to right) is a desaturated image, the unaltered image and a fully saturated image. The bottom row shows more subtle variations (left to right); slight desaturation, slight saturation and heavy saturation, but without the distortion of full saturation.

☞ see Hue 129, Saturation 218

Clarendon

Century Schoolbook (Bold)

Clarendon

Clarendon

A type of slab-serif font that appeared in Great Britain in 1820.
Clarendon is characterised by clear, objective and timeless forms,
and is legible in small point sizes.

☞ see Point Size 196

C   C M

C M Y   C M Y **K**

Cyan (C), magenta (M), yellow (Y) and black (K) are the subtractive primary inks, which are combined to reproduce the red, green and blue additive primaries in the four-colour printing process.

☞ see Additive & Subtractive Primaries 21, RGB 212

Understanding, knowing or interpretation based on what has been perceived, learned or reasoned. The cognitive interpretation of an image depends upon how it is presented. At a denotive level, all these pictures show a man. However, our interpretation of the man alters as the presentation of the image changes.

The first image (left) is bright and in colour and the man appears unthreatening, but when the image is reproduced as a dark monochromatic (centre), we interpret it differently, perhaps as being more sinister. The third image (right) is reproduced with a coarse halftone dot. Does this make the man appear friendly or unfriendly?

This text is set in Crud Font, a typographical choice that adds a cognitive value to the text and affects our interpretation of it.

☞ see Denotation 76, Halftone 125, Monochrome 166

An image creation technique characterised by the sticking together of paper, fabric, photographs or other media in unusual or surprising ways. Collage was popularised by Georges Braque and Pablo Picasso in the early twentieth century. Pictured is a design created by Why Not Associates that features a collage of text and colour blocks.

☞ see Montage 167

Different wavelengths of visible light. This broad definition of colour is further refined for graphic designers into the three characteristics that can be controlled and manipulated: hue, saturation and brightness.

Hue
Hue refers to the unique characteristic of a colour that helps us visually distinguish one colour from another. Hues are formed by different wavelengths of visible light.

Saturation
Saturation (or chroma) refers to the purity of a colour expressed by the amount of grey it has. At maximum saturation a colour contains no grey and such colours are described as 'vivid' or 'bright'. At lower saturation levels a colour contains increasing amounts of grey, which results in subdued and muted tones.

Brightness
Brightness of value refers to how dark a colour is. Brightness changes can be achieved by mixing a colour with different amounts of white or black.

Fonts can also be said to have colour due to the density of text on a page. Bookman occupies more white space and gives a dark colour while Helvetica Narrow occupies less space and gives a far lighter colour.

☞ see Chroma 52, Hue 129, Saturation 218

Describes those pages of a publication that will be printed with a
special colour or varnish as shown by colour coding on the imposition
plan. The use of different paper stocks can be shown on the imposition
plan in the same way.

Pictured below is a handbook created by NB Studios for Tate Modern.
The colour fall is restricted to those sections that printed on high-gloss
white stock and these are spliced between sections of uncoated
coloured stock, which print black and white to produce contrasting
tactile qualities.

☞ see Imposition 136

Pantone

The Pantone Colour Matching System (PMS) is a means of accurate colour reproduction within CMYK and Hexachrome printing processes, and allows designers to 'match' specific colours through the use of Pantone colour guides. The PMS system comprises a reference system for a gamut of colours that can be reproduced by combining various amounts of the process colour inks. PMS colours can also be applied as specially mixed spot colours.

Hexachrome

A six-colour process created by Pantone in 1994 that produces more effective purples, greens, oranges and flesh tones for accurate, vibrant and saturated colours. The Hexachrome system adds orange and green to the standard CMYK process colours. Hexachrome can reproduce 90 percent of the PMS colours.

CMYK

A four-colour process using the three trichromatic subtractive colour primaries (cyan, magenta and yellow) and black to reproduce colour images. CMYK can reproduce approximately 50 percent of the PMS colours.

RGB

Red, green and blue are the additive primaries that correspond to the primary colours of light. Graphic designers tend to use RGB images in their work in progress as images with three colour channels result in a smaller file size than those with four-channel CMYK. RGB files are then converted to CMYK upon completion of the design.

Lab

A colour model developed by the International Consortium on Illumination that defines colour values mathematically in order to facilitate consistent colour reproduction, regardless of the device producing it. The RGB and CMYK colour space systems do not define colour as such, but offer a mixing recipe for light or ink.

8-bit and 16-bit colour

The 8- and 16-bit colour systems are both methods for storing colour image information in a computer or image file. In the 8-bit system, each pixel is represented by one 8-bit byte that gives a maximum display of 256 colours at any one time (selected from a much wider palette). 16-bit colour allows up to 65,536 colours to be displayed at any one time.

Pictured is a fan of PMS colour matching cards

A circular representation of the colour spectrum. The colour wheel helps to explain the relationship between different colours within colour theory. The colour wheel also illustrates the classification of colours and provides a quick reference to the primary, secondary and tertiary hues, which can help a designer successfully select functional colour schemes.

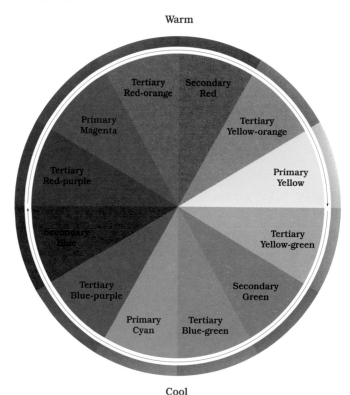

☞ see Additive & Subtractive Primaries 21, Tertiary Colours 247

C Colour Wheel Selections

A colour wheel can be drawn for any colour system (such as CMYK or RGB). They are used by artists, designers and other creatives to guide colour mixing.

Monochrome
Any single colour on the wheel.

Complementary
Colours that face each other on the wheel. These provide strong contrast and so their use will result in a more vibrant design. Also called contrasting colours.

Split complements
Three colours that comprise the two adjacent colours to the (unselected) colour that is complementary to the principal colour selection.

Triads
Triads are any three colours that are equidistant on the colour wheel. As all three colours contrast with one another, this provides a visual tension. The primary and secondary colour spaces are triads.

Analogous
The two colours on either side of a principal colour selection. Analogous colours provide a harmonious and natural blend.

Mutual complements
A triad of equidistant colours together with the complementary colour of the central one of the three.

Near complements
A colour adjacent to the complementary colour of the principal colour selection.

Double complements
Any two adjacent colours and their two complements.

☞ see CMYK 54, RGB 212

An area or field of a page layout into which text is flowed. Pictured is a spread created by Frost Design in which the columns are used to make a strong visual statement that is integral to the overall design.

☞ see Layout 146

Two or more parallel folds that alternate in opposite directions and open out like an accordion (a concertina is also called accordion fold).

Pictured here is a self-promotional calender created by Struktur design studio, which features a series of sections that are bonded together to form a concertina fold.

☞ see Folding 106

A modern art movement that originated in Moscow around 1920. Constructivism is characterised by the use of industrial materials, such as glass, sheet metal and plastic to create non-representational, often geometric objects, and its wide ranging commitment to total abstraction. Russian constructivism was influential to modernism through its use of black and red sans-serif typography, often arranged in asymmetrical blocks. Leading constructivist practitioners include Wassily Kandinsky, Alexander Rodchenko and El Lissitzky.

  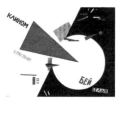

Pictured above is a self portrait by Russian avant-garde artist El Lissitzky (left); a poster for the Russian Exhibition in Zurich (centre), and *Beat the Whites With the Red Wedge,* a 1919 lithograph also by Lissitzky (right).

☛ see Asymmetry 32, Bauhaus 35

An implied uninterrupted connection between a given set of items, or items that form part of a coherent whole. Visual continuity means that image elements are grouped together and presented in a way that clearly shows that there is a connection between them, or that they are all representative of the same values. Continuity can be achieved through the use of colours and numerals as the pictured example shows.

see Colour 57, Identity 133, Numerals 173

The empty space inside the body of a stroke that is surrounded by the bowl. The counter is also called an eye for 'e', and a loop for the bowl created in the descender of a lower case 'g'. A counter can also describe the shape of the negative space within an open character, for example an upper case 'C'.

Pictured is a catalogue created by Why Not Associates for a show at the Royal Academy, which features title lettering with filled-in counters.

☞ see Type Anatomy 259

An adhesive-backed stock that has been kiss cut with a die so that elements of the design can be 'cracked' and separated from the substrate. Crack back is commonly used for sticker production.

Pictured is a publication created by Hat Trick Design that features a crack-back cover. Users are encouraged to remove the cover stickers and place them within the book.

☞ see Kiss Cut 144

When the inner folded pages of a publication (or printed section) extend further than the outer folded pages. Usually caused by the bulk of the paper or the extent of the publication.

Creep may not be a problem in saddle-stitched publications that are untrimmed, but information near the trim edge in perfect-bound publications may be lost if creep occurs so design elements need to be positioned away from the fore edge to ensure they are retained.

☞ see Perfect Binding 18, Binding 38

The means by which text of varying sizes aligns to the baseline grid. Pictured here, both texts, although different point sizes, cross align as they snap to the same grid. This main text is set on every other baseline while the secondary text is set on every baseline. The advantage of this system is that all lines align horizontally.

However the disadvantage is that in the main text, the leading is too loose, and in this secondary text it is too tight.

☞ see Baseline & Baseline Shift 34

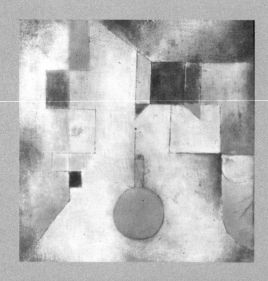

An art movement developed in Paris (1908–1914) and led by Pablo Picasso and Georges Braque. Cubism is characterised by the rejection of the single viewpoint. Subjects were fragmented and presented from different viewpoints at the same time. The movement also incorporated elements from African native art that was popular at the time and the new scientific theories of the age.

The second stage of cubism, called The Synthetic Phase (1913–1920s) saw a reduction of form to fewer elements with brighter colours used. This stage was typified by the works of Fernand Léger, Juan Gris and Piet Mondrian.

An art movement (1916–1920) of European writers and artists led by French poet Tristan Tzara. Characterised by the element of anarchic revolt and the role of chance in the creative process. Outraged by the carnage of the First World War, Dadaists aimed to shock people out of complacency with irreverence for the established norms.

Pictured is an interpretation of Marcel Duchamp's *LHOOQ*, a copy of Leonardo da Vinci's *Mona Lisa* embellished with graffiti, an act that encapsulates the Dadaist rejection of society's sacred cows. Leading Dadaists included Marcel Duchamp, Hans Arp and André Breton.

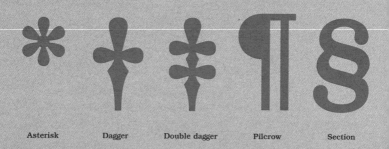

Asterisk   Dagger   Double dagger   Pilcrow   Section

One of five typographical symbols (above) used to indicate a footnote.
There is a governed order for the use of these symbols, and the dagger
is the second in the sequence. Once all five of the symbols in the
footnote hierarchy have been used, they can be 'doubled' to indicate
additional footnotes.

‡‡ Doubled double dagger
This is the eighth footnote symbol and it is used when the original five
symbols and the doubled dagger have been referenced.

☞ see Hierarchy 127

A design stamped into a substrate, without ink or foil, to give a recessed impression.

Pictured is a fashion show invitation created by Studio Thomson. It features a geometric font that is debossed into a textured stock, which provides defined, stylised shadows.

☞ see Emboss 92

The ragged edge of the paper as it leaves the papermaking machine. The deckle edge can be used to great decorative book detailing effect when not cut away. Machine-made paper has two deckle edges while handmade paper has four. The effect can be imitated by tearing the edge of the paper by hand. Note the uneven, textured edge on the pages of the example pictured. Also called feather edge.

☞ see Book Detailing 43

A term coined by French philosopher Jacques Derrida in the 1960s, deconstruction describes a method of critical enquiry that examines how meaning is constructed by challenging prescribed values which are presented to us. For example, why should folio numbers be small and in the corner of a page? Why can't they be large and in the centre of a page? Other creative movements such as modernism and postmodernism have also questioned how we look at the world and apportion meaning to things.

this is page 75

D Deconstruction

The literal and primary meaning of an image or graphic. The denotation of the image above is a picture of a woman, and nothing more or less. The cognitive interpretation is a secondary level within which we can extract more from the meaning of the image, such as what she is doing, how old she is, or where she is situated.

☞ see Cognition 55

F-stop settings on a camera

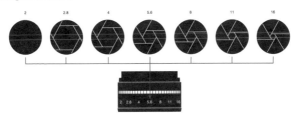

The zone of sharpest focus in front of and behind the main subject of a picture. Depth of field creates a sense of distance or perspective in a photograph. The above image has a very narrow depth of field, with only the foreground in focus. The depth of field will vary depending on the focal length of a camera lens, which is measured in millimetres. The shorter the focal length, the greater the depth of field. A camera lens includes a dial with settings (or F-stop numbers) that represent fractions of its focal length. These values determine how much light will enter the lens by increasing or decreasing the diameter of the aperture as illustrated above. Also called depth of focus.

☞ see Perspective 189

A print finishing process to cut away a part of the substrate using a steel die. Mainly used for decorative purposes, a die cut can enhance the visual impact of a design through the creation of interesting shapes, apertures or edges.

Pictured is a bookmark created by Studio Myerscough for a property development company that is die cut to the shape of a floor plan of one of the company's projects. Its abstract shape helps make a striking and distinctive product.

Various utility characters, symbols, bullets and graphic ornaments used in typography, including the printers' hand that is used throughout this publication to indicate references to other entries.

Woodtype Ornaments are decorative characters.

α β χ δ ε φ γ η ι φ κ λ μ ν ο π θ ρ σ τ υ ϖ ω ξ ψ ζ

Symbol includes Greek characters that are often used in mathematical formulae.

Textile are symbols used for washing instructions.

Hoefler Ornaments are decorative characters that can be used to form borders.

Zapf Dingbats are a range of bullets and other symbols.

☞ see Typefaces & Fonts 261

A specially drawn typeface for use on German road signage, which is printed in yellow and reversed out of black. The DIN-Schrift letterforms were later adjusted to improve clarity under adverse weather conditions. Alterations included making the counter of the 'o' more oval, lengthening letters to improve visual impact and changing the umlaut into a circular form rather than square. Pictured below are panels showing the typeface before and after the adjustments, and how these look under adverse viewing conditions (below right).

Before

After

☞ see Diacritical Marks 82, Reverse Out 211

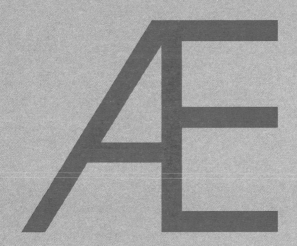

A special form of ligature in which two vowels are joined to form a single character such as the 'ae' that may be used in 'formulae'. Most fonts typically contain common diphthong characters.

☛ see Ligatures 151, Typefaces & Fonts 261

A type of punctuation typically placed above or below a letter to indicate modified pronunciation. Pictured are the main diacritical marks used in European languages.

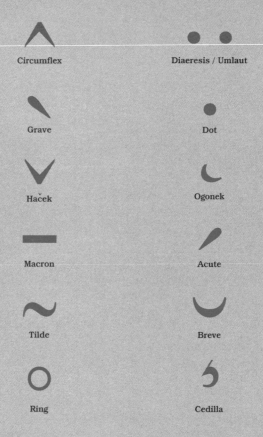

Circumflex	Diaeresis / Umlaut
Grave	Dot
Haček	Ogonek
Macron	Acute
Tilde	Breve
Ring	Cedilla

☞ see Accents 20

Subordinate
A visually weaker colour that complements or contrasts with the dominant colour.

Accent
A colour that is used to provide a sympathetic visual detail.

Dominant
The principle colour that is used to capture the viewer's attention.

Pictured is an interior created by Claire Gordon Interiors. Note how the dark, dominant colour attracts attention first, and contrasts with the accent colour, while the subordinate colour fulfils a balancing and supporting role. Colour schemes are often chosen through the use of colour wheels.

☞ see Colour Wheel Selections 61

The level of detail in the reproduction of an electronic image depends upon its resolution; the amount of information that it contains. With more information, the higher the resolution, and the better the quality and the more detailed the reproduction will be. Although similar, DPI, PPI and LPI refer to separate measurement methods, although in practice they tend to be used interchangeably. For example when people refer to a 300dpi image they usually mean a 300ppi image.

DPI (dots per inch)
A measure of how many ink dots a printer can deposit within an inch. For offset lithographic printing, a resolution of 300dpi is standard, although higher quality print jobs will demand higher values.

PPI (pixels per inch)
A reference to the number of pixels displayed both vertically and horizontally in each square inch of a digital image. This is a reflection of how much information an image contains.

LPI (lines per inch)
A measure of the number of cells in a halftone grid, which is used to convert continuous tone images (such as photographs) into halftone dots for printing. The more lines an image has the higher the level of detail it will contain. A low LPI value implies fewer cells and the halftone dots will appear more obvious in the printed image.

Enlarged initial capitals that drop down a specified number of lines into a paragraph.

Drop capitals create a strong visual starting point for a paragraph due to the hole they punch into the text block. This paragraph begins with a three-line drop capital.

Decorative capitals can be formed by using a different font for the drop cap, such as the swash character that starts this paragraph. The use of decorative capitals was common in medieval illuminated manuscripts.

Standing or pop capitals are enlarged initial capitals that sit on the baseline of the text. They create a strong visual point at the start of a paragraph due to the white space that they generate.

☞ see Swash Characters 245

A tonal image produced using black and one of the other subtractive primaries. In essence a duotone is akin to a black-and-white photograph in which the white tones have been replaced by another process colour.

Reducing colour detail to two tones allows images with different colour information to be presented in a consistent manner. As the colours can be altered independently results can vary from the subtle to the very graphic.

Duotone of black and yellow in equal amounts

Saturation of yellow

Duotone of yellow and magenta

Duotone of cyan and magenta

☞ see Additive & Subtractive Primaries 21, Quadtone 202, Tritone 257

A PROCESS WHEREBY TWO DIFFERENT MATERIALS ARE BONDED TOGETHER TO PRODUCE A SUBSTRATE THAT HAS DIFFERENT COLOURS ON EACH SIDE. WHILE A DUPLEXING EFFECT CAN BE ACHIEVED THROUGH DUPLEX PRINTING (PRINTING ON BOTH SIDES OF THE PAPER) THE END RESULT DOES NOT HAVE THE SAME COLOUR QUALITY AS USING DIFFERENT COLOURED STOCKS. THE USE OF DUPLEXING ALSO ALLOWS SUBSTRATE WEIGHT TO GO BEYOND THAT OF STANDARD STOCKS. THESE PROMOTIONAL CARDS WERE CREATED BY PARENT DESIGN. DUPLEXING WAS USED SO THAT THE STOCKS AND PRINTING INKS MIRRORED EACH OTHER. THE INKS USED WERE PMS SPECIALS RATHER THAN STANDARD PROCESS COLOURS

☞ see Special Colours 231

rg

An extending serif stroke that thickens at the terminal. Found on the lower case 'g' and 'r' on most serif typefaces. Pictured are letters with a dot-style ear, although they can also be chiselled.

☞ see Serif & Sans Serif 223, Type Anatomy 259

AN IMAGE THAT IS COMPOSED OF ELEMENTS DRAWN FROM VARIOUS SOURCES. DERIVING FROM THE GREEK **EKLEKTIKOS**, WHICH MEANS 'TO SELECT'.

ECLECTIC DESCRIBES THE USE OF SEVERAL INDIVIDUAL ELEMENTS, FROM A VARIETY OF SOURCES, SYSTEMS, OR STYLES TO CREATE AN IMAGE. THIS IMAGE WAS CREATED BY STUDIO OUTPUT FOR A MANCHESTER NIGHTCLUB.

THE IMAGE IS REMINISCENT OF DUTCH PAINTER HIERONYMUS BOSCH'S STYLE (1450–1516) WHOSE IMAGES INCLUDED WONDROUS, UNNATURAL ANIMALS AND OTHER SURREALIST CONSTRUCTIONS.

☞ see Surrealism 241

A sans-serif typeface style that developed after the introduction of William Caslon's Egyptian. Caslon introduced his typeface in response to public interest in Egypt following the campaign of Napoleon Bonaparte in 1798–1801. Arguably the first sans-serif typeface, Egyptian was not well received by the public and was called grotesque and gothic (a style of architecture going through a revival at the time). Egyptian has since become a term that refers to a range of slab-serif typefaces, perhaps because the slabs mirror the lines of the pyramids.

This page uses Memphis, a slab-serif Egyptian font.

☞ see Typefaces & Fonts 261

News Gothic has a square ellipsis...

...while Baskerville has a round version

A punctuation mark formed by a series of three periods or dots. Used in text to indicate an omission or incomplete statement, such as when contracting a quotation. From the Greek *ellipsis* that means 'a falling short or defect'. Used at the end of a sentence, the ellipsis is followed by a full stop. A true ellipsis has tighter points than a generated ellipsis and as it is a single unit, it will not split like the generated version. The dots may be square or round depending upon the font.

The *a*
Looking *pocket*
Book *history*
of
Circle
Press
1967-96

Cathy Courtney

A design stamped into a substrate, without ink or foil, to give a raised impression.

Pictured is a spread created by design studio Thomas Manss & Company for Circle Press that features an emboss of a reclining female nude. This adds a tactile element and gives the book a feel of sculptural beauty.

see Deboss 73

Ems

A typographical unit used for relative measurements. An em is a
unit of measurement derived from the width of the square body of
the metal cast majuscule 'M', and equals the size of a given type.
For example, 10pt type has a 10pt em.

Ens

Another relative measurement, an en is half of an em. Neither ems nor
ens have anything to do with the size of the 'M' or 'N' characters as
some characters extend beyond the limits of both measurements.

Hyphens

Both the em and en are very specific pieces of punctuation and should
not be confused with a hyphen, although they are all linked. An en is
half of an em while a hyphen is one third of an em.

Em   En   Hyphen

☞ see Absolute & Relative Measurements 18

An extended set of special characters that accompany a particular typeface. Expert sets include a range of characters that are not part of the usual typeface set such as ligatures, fractions, small capitals, the dotless 'i' and lining numerals. The addition of an expert set gives a designer greater control over text presentation and helps solve some of the common typographical problems that standard character sets present. This text is set in Janson, which has its own set of expert characters.

ABCDEFGHIJKLMNOPQRSTUVWXYZ
abcdefghijklmnopqrstuvwxyz
123456790!@£$%^&*(),.?':::

Janson

ABCDEFGHIJKLMNOPQRSTUVWXYZ
123456790fflfflffi¼½⅛⅜⅝⅓⅞

Janson Expert

☞ see Numerals 173, Small Capitals 230, Typefaces & Fonts 261

From *cadavre exquis*; a surrealist technique that uses chance and accident in the creation of text or pictures. Pictured is a brochure created by KesselsKramer for the Hans Brinker Budget Hotel in Amsterdam. The brochure features cross-cut pages that can be independently turned, and works as an exquisite corpse by the juxtaposition of images, which depict how guests appear before and after their stay at the hotel.

see Juxtaposition 142, Surrealism 241

The number of pages in a printed publication. Typically the number of pages is determined at the start of the design stage so that print costs can be calculated in advance and the content is then made to fit. This volume for instance has an extent of 288 pages and the content has been developed to fit this specification. Book manuscripts are often 'cast-off' whereby the content is roughly flowed into a layout to provide an estimate of what the extent will be.

☞ see Layout 146

A numerical series where each number is the sum of the preceding two numbers in the sequence. Fibonacci numbers are named after mathematician Fibonacci, or Leonardo of Pisa who observed this sequence in the proportions of the natural world. Numbers from the Fibonacci sequence are used in the golden section to produce proportionally beautiful page sizes.

Pictured is a Fibonacci spiral, which can be created by drawing quarter circles through a set of Fibonacci squares. The ratio of the sides of Fibonacci squares is 8:13, which are two consecutive numbers in the Fibonacci sequence.

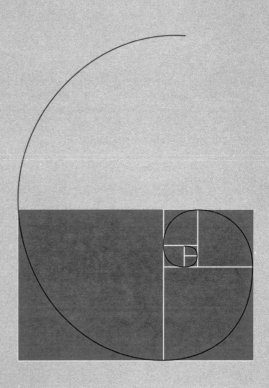

0+1=1
1+1=2
1+2=3
2+3=5
3+5=8
5+8=13
8+13=21
13+21=34
21+34=55
34+55=89
55+89=144
89+144=233…

☞ see Golden Section 116

Any of several methods for storing digital images. Common file formats include bitmap, EPS, JPEG and TIFF.

Scalability
Encapsulated PostScript (EPS) is a picture file format for storing vector or object-based artwork and bitmaps. EPS files can be resized, distorted and colour separated, but no content alteration can usually be made. Above left is an EPS image file that has been enlarged with no degradation in image quality. The TIFF image file (shown above right), suffers pixelation at the same enlargement value.

Sharing
JPEG images are compressed to discard image information, which reduces their file size and makes them easier to send to other people via email. They are suitable for images with complex pixel gradations, but not for flat colour.

Altering
A TIFF file is a flexible method for storing halftones and photographic images and can be easily manipulated by appropriate software. Simple adjustments can also be easily made to bitmap images, as the examples below demonstrate.

☞ see Bitmap 31, Pixel 193

Intricate ornamental work that is typically produced in gold, silver or other fine wire. Pictured is the packaging for the Rolling Stones' *Bridges to Babylon* CD created by Stefan Sagmeister and Hjalti Karlsson. It features an illustration of an Assyrian lion by Kevin Murphy that is emphasised by a filigree slipcase, which outlines the drawing in intricate detail.

☞ see Outline 177

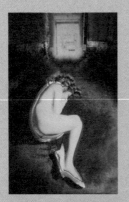

A device used to filter light of specific wavelengths in order to change the presentation of a final image, whether a photograph or digital file. A filter can make an adjustment that is so subtle, the viewer barely recognises the enhancement (such as refining an image to create an opal blue sky or coral sand beach). But filters can also be used to make dramatic and graphic interventions, as can be seen in this image (left). A plethora of filters are available as part of image manipulation and photo-editing programs, and some can produce some interesting and startling graphic effects as shown below.

Solarisation
A photographic effect whereby some tones of an image are reversed, and highlights are added to outlines for emphasis. This effect can be achieved in photo-editing software, or by briefly (over-) exposing the image to light, then washing and redeveloping it.

Spherize
The edges of an image can be warped into a circular construction through the use of a fisheye, spherize, or warp filter in most photo-editing programs. This approximates the effect that can be obtained with a fisheye camera lens.

Colour halftone
A halftone filter simulates the halftone dots that are used for photographic reproduction in the printing process. This filter can be used to create various graphic effects.

☞ see Halftone 125, Noise 172

The extensions of the cover stock or book's dust jacket, which are folded back into the publication to add additional support and rigidity. Flaps often contain notes about the book or its author. Shown here is the cover of this book with its flaps as a flat artwork. Note that the flaps are slightly shorter than the text box so that they can fold in without causing bowing on the cover.

☞ see Book Detailing 43

Fine woollen refuse or vegetable fibre dust that is fixed with glue or size to a substrate to provide a velvety or cloth-like appearance.

Flock adds a tactile and alternative visual element to a design and while it does not provide a good surface to print upon, it can be used to good decorative effect with foil-blocking, as this example shows.

Pictured below is a catalogue created by Faydherbe / De Vringer for the typeface Dolly, which was created by Underwear. The product's logo, a dog called Dolly, is foil-blocked on to the catalogue's flocked cover.

☞ see Typefaces and Fonts 261

FLOOD COLOUR

A full-bleed colour that flows off every side of the printed piece. When colour runs off the sides of the page it is visible on the outer edge of a publication (in a similar way as fore-edge printing, although without the intensity). As such, flood printing can be a useful way of colour coding sections of a publication when the use of different stocks is not an option.

☞ see Book Detailing 43, Stock 237

A vibrant special colour that cannot be reproduced by combining the standard process colours.

Pictured below is a brochure created by Rose Design for publisher Fourth Estate, which uses green fluorescent ink to represent a highlighter pen.

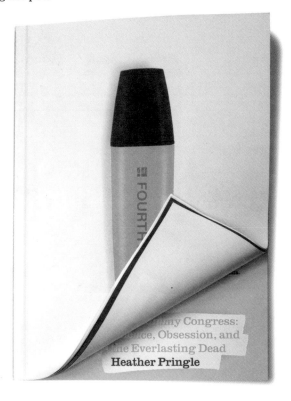

☞ see Colour 57

A print-finishing material that is stamped onto a substrate using a
heated die. This technique is also called foil block, block print or hot
foil stamp. Pictured above is the cover of a publication created by
The Kitchen to celebrate the tenth anniversary of London nightclub,
The End. It features an illustration of the club entrance by Will Barras
that is foil blocked in blue onto a greyboard stock.

☞ see Stock 237

A print finishing process whereby pages are creased and doubled in various combinations to produce a signature for binding. Folding methods produce a variety of results and serve different purposes, as the examples pictured below illustrate.

An **accordion** or **concertina fold** comprises two or more parallel folds that run in opposite directions, and open out like an accordion.

A **roll fold** comprises two or more parallel folds which go in the same direction so that the panels fold in on themselves and nest within one another. The page widths of each panel may be made incrementally smaller so that they can nest more comfortably.

A **harmonica self-cover fold** comprises two panels that form a cover and encase the other folded panels. The first two panels need to be larger than the others to allow for creep.

A **double gatefold** has three panels extending out from both the recto and verso pages. These panels fold in towards the centre of the publication with an accordion fold.

☞ see Concertina 63, Gatefold 114, Roll Fold 215

A special process for printing on the cut edges of a perfect bound publication. Originally, this process was performed to provide added protection to books that were likely to suffer high usage, such as bibles and ledgers, but it has since been adopted as a means to add additional decorative touches to a design, such as the black edges of this brochure by Studio Myerscough for London-based MAK Architects (above).

☞ see Book Detailing 43, Perfect Binding 187

K CMYK

A black that is produced using all four of the CMYK process colours. The use of the four process colours results in a deeper, richer black than if the black was printed as a single colour, as shown above. By varying the CMYK values used, the warmth of a black can be altered. For example, using less magenta and yellow gives a bluer black, while using less cyan gives a warmer black.

☞ see CMYK 54, Shiner 224

A vertical fold immediately followed by a horizontal fold, which forms a
four-page uncut section. French folds are typically printed on only one
side, as the inner pages will not be seen when the sections are bound.
A French fold can be bound into a publication to provide a section that
has a more substantial feel due to the doubled page. In this example
(above) by North Design for ImageBank, the section is sewn through
the (open) binding edge so that the fore and top edges remained folded
and untrimmed. The top edge was then trimmed off to leave a sealed
fore edge, which formed a cavity between the pages.

☞ see Folding 106

A technique for mural painting in which water-borne pigment is applied to a damp lime-plaster surface. The colours penetrate the plaster and then become fixed as it dries. Meaning 'fresh' in Italian, fresco painting was used by Michaelangelo to decorate many religious buildings in Renaissance Italy. More recently, it has been used by artists such as Diego Rivera. Pictured below is a ceiling fresco at El Escorial in Spain.

☞ see Mural 170

A decorated or sculptured horizontal element in architecture that
forms part of an entablature between the architrave and cornice.
While similar to a mural, a frieze typically adds a decorative element
at the top of a building. Pictured is *The Triumph of Arts and Sciences*;
the terracotta frieze that surrounds London's Royal Albert Hall.

Light

23	24	25	26	27	28
33	34	35	36	37	38
43	44	45	46	47	48
53	54	55	56	57	58
63	64	65	66	67	68
73	74	75	76	77	78
83	84	85	86	87	88
93	94	95	96	97	98

Black

Extended

Condensed

A font numbering system developed by Adrian Frutiger to identify the width and weight of a typeface family. The diagrammatic presentation of Frutiger's grid provides a sense of order and homogeneity through the visual relationships of weight and width, which allows for the harmonious selection of type.

Helvetica 25   **Helvetica 95**

☞ **see Italic & Oblique 141, Typefaces & Fonts 261**

The spectrum of colours that scanners, monitors, software applications and printing processes can reproduce. The gamut defines the range of colours that are at the designer's disposal. Using colours at the fringes of the gamut will mean it will be difficult to ensure they remain faithful to the original design if it is transferred from one device to another.

Pictured below is a gamut diagram in which the red line represents the Hexachrome gamut, the blue line represents the RGB gamut, and the green line represents the CMYK gamut. The outer black line denotes the spectral colour gamut.

In this illustration the black outer line depicts the full spectral colour gamut.

The red line denotes the extent of the Hexachrome system, which adds orange and green to increase the gamut.

The green line shows the limits of the CMYK gamut, and the blue line shows the reach of the RGB gamut range. RGB displays approximately 70 percent of the colours perceived by the human eye and CMYK even less.

☞ see CMYK 54, Colour 57, RGB 212

A type of fold in which the right- and left-hand pages of a four-panel sheet fold inward and meet in the middle of the page without overlapping. Gatefolds are typically used to provide more space for pictures or other graphic content in magazines and brochures. Pictured is a spread from a brochure created by SEA Design for Staverton. It features a four-panel gatefold showcasing the clean lines of the product.

☞ see Folding 106

Images, designs, layouts and typographic letterforms based on simple geometric shapes such as the circle, square, triangle and trapezoid. Geometric fonts, such as those created by the Bauhaus in the early twentieth century, tend to possess uniform stroke width and fully rounded characters. This geometric font is Century Gothic; notice the uniform nature of its characters.

☞ see Ascenders & Descenders 31, Bauhaus 35, Humanist 130

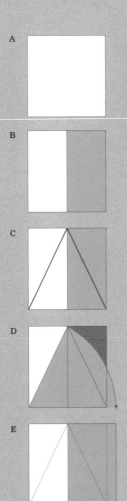

A

B

C

D

E

The approximate 8:13 ratio that was thought by the ancients to represent infallibly beautiful proportions. The golden section forms the basis of some paper sizes due to the harmonious proportions it provides, and its principles can be used as a means of achieving balanced designs.

Pictured is the sequence for drawing a golden section. To form a golden section begin with a square (A) and dissect it (B). Then form an isosceles triangle (C) by drawing lines from the bottom corners to the top of the bisecting line. Next, extend an arc from the apex of the triangle to the baseline (D) and draw a line perpendicular to the baseline from the point at which the arc intersects it. Complete the rectangle to form a golden section (E).

☞ see Fibonacci Numbers 97

A colour fill that increases in intensity from white through various tonal gradations to solid colour, or from one colour to another.

Pictured is an identity created by Form Design that uses a multicolour gradient to imply variety, diversity and interest.

see Colour 57

Deriving from the Italian *graffito*, which means a scratching or scribble, graffiti is a plural noun used to describe unauthorised writings or drawings on public surfaces. Graffiti can encompass everything from tags scrawled on buses and initials spray painted on walls, to other personal forms of communication that are an ever present component of modern urban life.

Pictured above is an example of graffiti produced using a stencil, which gives a hard, dramatic and almost industrial feel.

☞ see Mark Making 157

A term that describes a visual effect in photography that is caused by the large grain size of fast-speed films reacting to light. Larger grain size means less image detail is captured, but this can lend a photograph an artistic grittiness, particularly in black-and-white photography. Grain can also be produced by using image manipulation software, and in digital terms this is referred to as 'noise'.

☞ see Noise 171

An image that contains shades of grey as well as black and white. Also the brightness of a pixel, expressed as a value representing its lightness from black to white. A greyscale image can be coloured, turned into a negative, or otherwise altered by adjusting its contrast or other controls in image-manipulation programs.

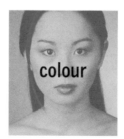

A graphic structure used to organise the placement of individual elements within a design or page. A grid (or baseline grid) serves a similar function to the scaffolding used in building construction and acts as a positioning guide for text, pictures, diagrams, charts, folios, strap lines, columns and so on.

A is a double column into which text is flowed. Columns provide a strong sense of order to body text, but they can also result in static designs where there is little variation or few opportunities to pursue alternative text presentation techniques.

B is the head (or top) margin. This the space at the top of the page. Here, the head margin carries a running title and is half the height of the foot margin.

C is the foot margin. This is usually the largest margin on the page. In this example, the bottom margin is twice the width of the head margin.

D is the back edge or inside margin, which is commonly the narrowest page margin. The inside margin is traditionally half the size of the outer margin.

E is the fore edge or outer margin at the trim edge of the page. Here it is used as a space for notes and captions. These have been differentiated by the use of italics and positioned to align horizontally with body text.

F marks the position of the folio or page numbers. These are traditionally placed at the outer edge of the bottom margin where they add dynamism because they are more noticeable. However, placing folios in the centre of the text block is considered harmonious.

G is a running title (or header, running head or strap line). This is a repeated line of text that appears on each page of a book. A running title usually appears at the top of the page although they can be placed at the foot or in the side margin. The folio number is often incorporated into the running head.

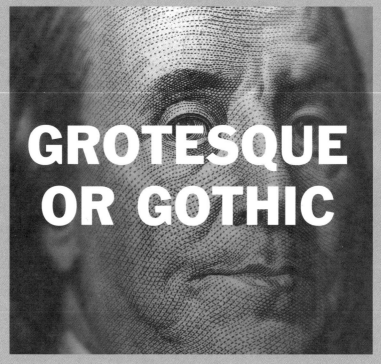

GROTESQUE OR GOTHIC

Grotesque typefaces began to be developed in the early nineteenth century following the introduction of William Caslon's Egyptian type. Caslon's typeface was not well received and was described as 'grotesque' and 'gothic' (comments influenced by a style of architecture experiencing a revival at the time). Pictured is US President Benjamin Franklin, after whom Franklin Gothic, the font this page uses, was named. Franklin Gothic was created by Morris Fuller Benton in 1904.

☞ see Typefaces & Fonts 261

A weight/area measurement used
to specify printing paper. GSM is
an abbreviation for grams per
square metre.

In the ISO paper system, an
A1 sheet has an area of 1 square
metre and therefore its GSM
value refers to the weight
of a single A1 sheet.

☞ see ISO Paper Sizes 140

The sliver of a page at the binding margin. The gutter is
often nicked during binding, which means that anything
printed at this extreme edge of the page may not be visible.
Information can become lost or difficult to see, which is
exploited by Frost Design in the example above (in *Zembla*
magazine) for graphic effect. The gutter is also used to
describe the space between adjacent text columns.

☞ see Binding 38, Column 62

Dot pattern

Line pattern

Ellipse pattern

Square pattern

Coarse dot pattern

Coarse line pattern

An image formed from dots that is suitable for printing by the offset lithographic printing process. The halftone image is formed by using line screens to convert a continuous tone image (such as a photograph) into a composition of dots. Both the pattern, size and direction of the dots (or other shapes) can be changed and manipulated to achieve various creative effects. Digital halftone images are commonly stored as TIFF format files.

☞ see File Formats 98

The profession, study, history and classification of armorial bearings and the tracing of genealogies. Pictured above is the coat of arms of the Visconti family, who ruled in Milan, Italy, from 1277 to 1447.

A logical way to express the relative importance of different text elements by providing a visual guide to their organisation.

A text hierarchy helps makes a layout clear, unambiguous and easier to digest. A text hierarchy can be established in numerous ways by employing different weights, sizes and styles of a font.

Alternatively, a simple hierarchy can be achieved by using different colours of the same font.

☞ see Frutiger's Grid 112

A printing process whereby lines of type are cast in molten metal before being set for printing. Hot metal type or hot type composition afforded the creation of large quantities of type in a relatively inexpensive fashion and was used extensively by the newspaper industry. It has since been made obsolete by computer technology.

The colour reflected or transmitted from an object. Hue is expressed as a value between 0 and 360 on the colour wheel. Changing hue values will dramatically alter the colour of an image.

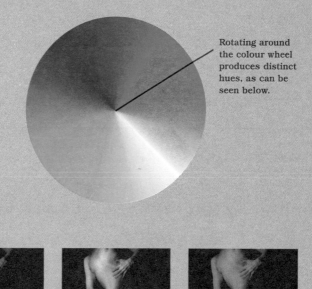

Rotating around the colour wheel produces distinct hues, as can be seen below.

☞ see Colour Wheel 60, Hue 129, Saturation 218

A class of sans-serif typefaces that are inspired by hand lettering rather than geometric forms. Humanist typefaces are the most calligraphic of sans-serif typefaces, which explains why they have been successfully used for body text where other sans-serif styles have failed. This page is set in Edward Johnston's Railway Type, which was designed for the London Underground.

☞ see Geometric 115

An artistic style that blends reality and representation to such an extent that it will not be clear where one stops and the other begins.

Hyperreal images are 'better' or 'improved' versions of reality. This is the graphic space where fantasy and reality collide. Famous hyperrealists include Jean Baudrillard, Daniel Boorstin and Umberto Eco.

For example, the top left image shows all the imperfections on the model's face. The top right image is a hyperreal version; the model's eyes are whiter, her skin is smoother and so on. Pictured right is a hyperreal image created by Studio Output for the Ministry of Sound.

A graphic element that represents an object, person or something else
by reducing it to simple and instant characteristics. Icons should not be confused
with symbols or pictograms. While most of the objects pictured below can be
recognised from their silhouettes, some (such as the pineapple and telephone)
contain too much detail, which diminishes their effectiveness as icons, whereas
the pipe, trophy and guitar are very effective.

Icon is also used as a collective term for a religious painting in oil on a small
wooden panel pertaining to the Orthodox Christian church of Eastern Europe.

see Pictogram 192, Symbols 242

The behavioural characteristics of a company, which define what qualities are synonymous with its level of service, its innovative nature or its approach to doing business. Branding is the expression or presence of this identity in the marketplace and can be used to create a unique identity.

If a company sells a range of complementary products, such as coffee and cakes, the use of an encompassing, monolithic brand may be suitable. If the product offerings are wildly different such as coffee and construction services, the use of one encompassing brand is incongruous and a multiple brand approach is usually more applicable. However, some brands, such as Virgin, have successfully developed a monolithic brand structure conveying a range of disparate products (such as airlines, finance services and soft drinks) with great success by carefully selecting product groups that share similar traits for its (essentially) single consumer base.

Monolithic identity
All companies/products carry
the same brand.

Endorsed identity
A separate brand is endorsed
by the parent company to
show its lineage.

Branded identity
A fully-branded product in its
own right, without reference to
the parent company.

☞ see Brand 45

A graphic symbol used to represent an idea. The word ideogram is commonly used to describe logographic writing systems such as Egyptian hieroglyphs (pictured) and the characters of Asiatic languages, such as Chinese and Japanese – although the symbols in these languages generally represent words or morphemes rather than pure ideas. Ideograms are often used in information design, including road and airport signage.

☞ see Pictogram 192, Symbols 242

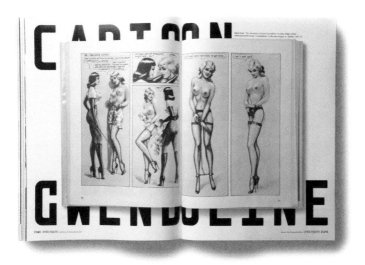

Artwork that explains, exemplifies or adorns. Illustration, whether by hand or by digital means, takes many forms and is used to convey an impression that the realism of photography cannot always provide. Ranging from the line work of Frost Design's spread from *Zembla* magazine (top) to the witty detail in the invitation created by Studio Thomson (above) where every line is crucial, or the intricate halftones in the example (right) by Studio Output, illustration can be used in a variety of ways.

☞ see Halftone 125, Line Art 152, Linocut 153

A plan showing the arrangement of a publication's pages in the sequence and position that they will appear when printed before being cut, folded and trimmed.

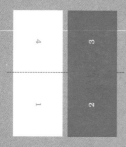

Printed pages back up. For example, in a book page two will be printed backed up by page three. Pages can be printed using different methods. The work and turn method allows both sides of the sheet to be printed using a single plate, which reduces cost. After the first printing pass, the paper is turned for a second pass. The gripper edge remains the same, but the side guides are different. The work and tumble imposition also allows a sheet to be printed using a single plate. In this instance, the stock is flopped after the first side is printed so that the trailing edge of the first pass becomes the gripper edge for the second pass. The same side guide is used for both passes. The work and twist method prints the same content twice on the same side of the sheet. Following the first pass, the sheet is turned and then printed again. These methods are suitable for small jobs such as a four-page brochure.

For larger or more complicated jobs, only half the pages are viewable on any one side of the sheet. In the example above, pages 1–16 print independently of pages 17–32, which means that if a special colour is used, it may only be printed on one side and may not be available to all pages. This gives a designer greater control over the colour fall or usage and also helps to reduce print costs.

☞ see Pagination 179, Special Colours 231

Describes the process of leaving a gap in the bottom ink layer so that any image printed over it (overlapping it) appears without colour modification from the base ink. Knockout, along with overprinting, are techniques that can be used to perform ink trapping.

Knockout
In the central square in the sequence above, a space has been knocked out of the cyan ink layer for another colour to fill, in this case magenta. The result is a magenta letter whose colour is not modified or affected by the cyan ink layer.

Overprint
An overprint produces a different effect. With no colour knocked out of the cyan ink, the magenta ink overprints it, which modifies the resulting colour of the letter.

☞ see CMYK 54, Overprint 178, Trapping 256

Ink Well

Exaggerated cuts in letters of a typeface that are intended to fill with ink during printing and help maintain character definition. Also called ink traps. Print-process control has advanced to the extent that these are now seldom needed, although many fonts still include them. Pictured is Bell Centennial, a font with exaggerated ink wells, created by Matthew Carter in 1976 for the American telephone company Bell.

☞ see Typefaces & Fonts 261

The use of capital letters within (rather than at the start of) words. Also called camel case due to the humped profile that results. InterCap words are typically those relating to trademarks or other similar constructs. The most obvious example in graphic design and printing is 'PostScript'.

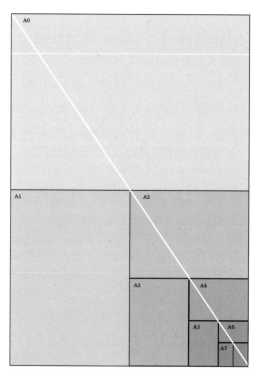

Standard paper sizes used throughout Europe and most of the world except the US and Canada. The modern ISO system is based on a width-to-height ratio of the square root of two (1:1.4142). Format AO has an area of one square metre. The ISO A series comprises a range of paper sizes that differ from the next size by a factor of 2 or 1/2. The B series sizes are intermediate sizes and the C series sizes are for envelopes that can contain A series stationery. RA and SRA are the sheet sizes from which A size paper can be cut.

A drawn typeface based around an axis that is angled somewhere between 7 and 20 degrees. Italics derived from the subtly angled calligraphic typefaces used in sixteenth century Italy, and cuts with this calligraphic form were drawn to accompany the upright Roman forms of serif typefaces. Italics such as Novarese, which is used here, sit compactly, in part due to their use of many ligatures. Novarese is based on older italic forms, but note that the upper case characters are standard Roman capitals.

Italic
True italic typefaces are specifically drawn and include characters that can be visually very different, such as the italic 'a' shown above.

Oblique
Obliques are slanted versions of the Roman font, and so are visually similar.

☞ see Type Classification 260

The placement of image items side by side to highlight or create a relationship between them, taken from the Latin *juxta*, which means near.

Pictured is a brochure created by Studio Myerscough. Its pages are printed as loose sheets and bound together, causing a juxtaposition of photographic details and atmospheric interior views.

☞ see Binding 38

Kerning is the manual or automated removal of space between letters
to improve the visual look of type. 'Kern' is a term that refers to those
parts of a metal type character which extend beyond the metal block,
such as the arm of an 'f' for instance. In the example below, the
unkerned 'K' is distant from the rest of the letters of the word, as is
the 'g'. Removing some of the space that separates these letters
through kerning enables a more natural visual balance to be found.
Kerning is typically used in conjunction with letterspacing.

Without kerning

Kerning

With kerning (the magenta values are the points subtracted)

Kerning

-7   -3   -3

☞ see Letterspacing 150, Type Anatomy 259

A die cutting method, often used with self-adhesive substrates, whereby the face stock is die cut, but not the backing sheet, to facilitate the easy removal of the cut stock. Pictured is a sticker pack created by NB: Studio.

A style that is considered to be overly sentimental and/or pretentious. Often draws upon mass culture and mass-produced items that may have formerly met with critical disdain. As fashions change, what was once kitsch becomes cool.

The arrangement of text, images and other visual elements in a design to resemble the final appearance of the piece. A layout is typically created within a structure such as a grid. A page layout has active and passive areas due to the way that the eye reads a page.

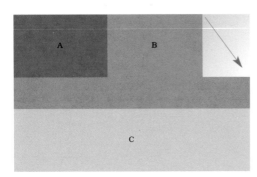

The illustration shows the levels of activity in different areas of a page. The darker areas are those grabbing most attention.

Pictured is a spread created by Frost Design. The image caption has been placed in a layout hotspot.

☞ see Grid 121

The space between lines of type measured from baseline to baseline. Leading is expressed in points and is a term that derives from hot metal printing, when strips of lead were placed between the lines of type to provide sufficient spacing. Pictured above is a spread created by Frost Design in which the title text has been set without any leading. Notice how the baseline has also become the ascender line.

☞ see Negative Leading 171

A printing technique that gives an image depth or motion as the viewing angle of it changes.

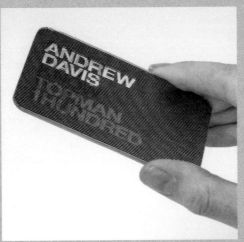

Lenticular printing alternates strips of several images onto the back of a transparent plastic sheet, which contains a series of curved ridges called lenticules. The strips are aligned so that those forming a specific image are refracted to the same point. Pictured is a piece of promotional material created by The Kitchen design studio for Topman and is a lenticular of a question and an answer.

A method of relief printing whereby a raised, inked surface is pressed against a substrate. Letterpress was the first commercial printing method as it allowed the production of high-volume print runs. As such it is the source of many printing terms used today. The raised surface that makes the impression is typically made from pieces of type, but photoengraved plates can also be used. Letterpress printing can be identified by the sharp and precise edges to letters and their heavier ink border.

A defect of letterpress is appealing to modern designers. When improperly inked, patches appear in the letters giving them a uniqueness, as each impression is subtly different. This effect can be used to evoke nostalgia for a bygone era, as seen in the pictured spread created by Frost Design, which features an image of an oversize letterpressed numeral '3'. Letterpress also leaves a slight indentation in the stock giving a tactile element to a design, particularly when a heavier substrate is selected.

☛ see Stock 237

The insertion of space between characters to produce harmonious and balanced typesetting. Some fonts require more letterspacing than others due to their type characteristics. For example, the exaggerated serifs of Clarendon, pictured below, require more letterspacing so that the letterforms do not collide. Designers typically use a combination of letterspacing and kerning to produce a tidy text block.

Without **kerning**

Trap

With **letterspacing** (the magenta values are the points added)

Trap

+15   +5

☞ see Kerning 143, Type Anatomy 260

A typographical device that joins two or three separate type characters together to form a single unit and prevent characters from interfering with one another.

fi fl ff ffi ffl   fi fl ff ffi ffl   fi fl

Normal type   Ligatures   Logotypes

Proper ligatures are characters that are drawn for use as a unit and are included with many fonts, particularly expert sets. Some sans-serif fonts (above, far right) have characters that perform the same function as ligatures, but as they do not join they are, strictly speaking, logotypes. Pictured below is a design by Parent with linked letterforms, although strictly speaking, these are not ligatures; they perform a similar task, linking individual units into a whole.

A monotone picture drawn only as lines and without colour
filling or shading. A line-art image reduces the visual impression
to the essential information without any distractions.

Pictured above is a line art illustration created by Vasava Artworks for a cover
of *Uno* magazine. This image has been partially coloured to highlight the eyes
of the subject.

☞ see Illustration 135

A relief print made with a design that has been cut into linoleum. Lino-cut printing employs the same principles as woodcut printing, but linoleum is easier to cut and prints more evenly. The relief print image will be the reverse of the design that is cut into the linoleum. Pictured above is a lino-cut design created by Laura Neal.

A printing process that uses the repulsion of oil and water to ink a plate which contains a design. Lithography means 'writing on stone' and was discovered by Alois Senefelder around 1798 in Prague. Its working principle is the basis of the offset lithographic printing process, which made four-colour printing available on an industrial scale. Four-colour printing entails reproducing colour images as a series of four plates, each of which corresponds to the cyan, magenta, yellow and black process colours.

The CMYK printing sequence is pictured in the top row below. This order can be changed to produce different visual results. The bottom row (left to right) features an unaltered four-colour image, an image that prints the magenta and cyan plates in the wrong order, a yellow plate printing in place of all four colours, and an image with the black plate missing, which produces a lighter, less contrasted image.

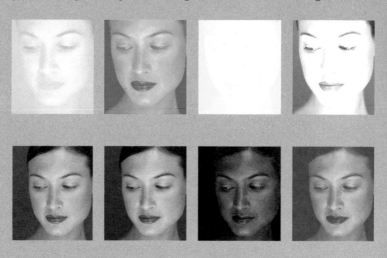

☞ see CMYK 54

Logos

A graphic symbol that is designed to represent the character of a company, product or service or other entity. Pictured here is the logo used to represent the work of the World Wildlife Fund as it seeks to protect endangered species such as the Giant Panda.

Logotypes

Logotypes function by literally identifying the organisation they refer to, using characters styled in such a way as to give an indication of its strengths or culture.

Gifts

Pictured here is the Federal Express logo created by Landor Associates and it works on two levels. At first glance it is just a simple contraction of the company's name. But some logos work incredibly hard, and this one carries a subliminal secondary message; notice the arrowhead created between the 'E' and 'X'. This helps enforce the nature of FedEx's business: fast and direct delivery.

☞ see Brand 45

CAPITAL LETTERS. ALSO CALLED UPPER CASE LETTERS BECAUSE IN THE DAYS OF LETTERPRESS PRINTING, MAJUSCULES WERE KEPT IN THE UPPER BOX OR CASE OF TYPE. THIS TEXT IS SET IN TRAJAN BOLD.

Lower case Letters that originally derived from carolingian characters. this text is set in camellia. the majority of fonts contain both majuscule and minuscule character sets, however, some fonts are unicase: they only have one case.

☞ see Typefaces & Fonts 261

A means of creating type or an image by hand. Mark making or hand-drawn type is a means of adding raw immediacy to a design. Pictured above is a spread created by Frost Design for *Zembla* magazine that features a hand-drawn panel with scrawled lettering, which invokes the era of punk music and punk fanzines.

☞ see Illustration 135, Linocut 153, Typefaces & Fonts 261

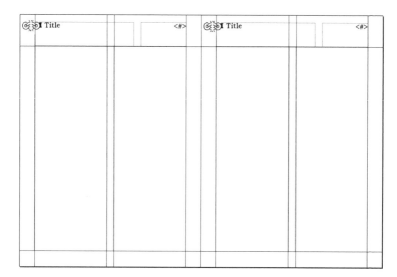

In the context of layout software applications, the template pages that contain common elements will appear throughout a document. A document can use different master pages for different sections. For example, one section could have a two-column right-hand master page while another section has a three-column right-hand master page. Any content that is placed or altered on a master page will appear on all the pages that the master page governs. The symbol in the top right corner of both master pages is an automatic page number, which means that if you change the order of the publication the page numbers will automatically update.

The length of a line of text. There are several methods for calculating the measure of a particular font, although the length that results from any of these will depend upon the point size used. The width of the lower case alphabet can be used as a reference; the measure is usually between 1.5–2 times this width. This calculation gives a comfortable type measure that is not so short as to cause awkward returns or gaps, and not so long as to be uncomfortable to read. Note that as type size decreases, so does the optimum measure width.

abcdefghijklmnopqrstuvwxyz

Times New Roman

abcdefghijklmnopqrstuvwxyz

Bookman Old Style

A more complex method is to make a measurement in picas. There should be a relationship of 2:1 to 2.5:1 between the measure in picas and the typesize in points. For example, a 16–20 pica measure for 8pt type, 20–25 picas for 10pt type and 24–30 picas for 12pt type.

Another simple formula is to specify the number of characters per line (not less than 25, or more than 70), for example 40, which is enough for about six words of six characters per line.

Type with a narrow set width will look different to text set with a wide set width. Changing the typeface will alter the width setting and may call for adjustment of the measure. While one type may give a relatively comfortable fit in the measure, another may have awkward spacing issues, particularly in justified text, as shown here.

Type with a narrow set width will look different to text set with a wide set width. Changing the typeface will alter the width setting and may call for adjustment of the measure. While one type may give a relatively comfortable fit in the measure, another may have awkward spacing issues, particularly in justified text, as shown here.

☞ see Alignment 22

A method of reducing the values of an image to remove detail without causing pixelation.

see Filters 100

A highly reflective ink or foil with metallic characteristics. Metallic
inks are special printing inks, which are outside of the standard
gamut of the CMYK or Hexachrome colour spaces. These colours
can also be applied to a design through the use of a foil stamp.
Pictured is a brochure by SEA Design that features text produced
with a metallic foil.

☞ see CMYK 54, Gamut 113

A device that transfers meaning from one thing to another even though there may not be a close relationship between them. A visual metaphor conveys an impression that is relatively unfamiliar by drawing a comparison with something familiar.

☞ see Metonym 163, Synecdoche 244

Something that denotes one thing, but is used to refer to something else. The viewer creates an association between the object and its intended meaning, rather than its literal meaning. The taxi cabs above are a metonym of New York, they are part of the city, but not the city itself.

☞ see Metaphor 162, Synecdoche 244

Form follows function

Modernism (1890–1940) through the cubist, surrealist and Dadaist movements was shaped by the industrialisation and urbanisation of Western society. Modernists, including the De Stijl, constructivism and Bauhaus movements, departed from the rural and provincial zeitgeist prevalent in the Victorian era, rejecting its values and styles in favour of cosmopolitanism.

Functionality and progress, expressed through the maxim of 'form follows function' became key concerns in the attempt to move beyond the external physical representation of reality through experimentation in a struggle to define what should be considered 'modern'.

In graphic design, modernism embraced an asymmetrical approach to layout with strict adherence to the grid, an emphasis on white space and sans-serif typography, and the absence of decoration and embellishment.

see Asymmetry 32
see Bauhaus 35
see Constructivism 64
see Grid 121
see Layout 146
see White Space 267
see Zeitgeist 271

Printed patterns produced by colour halftone dots that are created when the screen angles of the different printing plates interfere. Images are reproduced using four (CMYK) halftone screens that are set at different angles so that the production of a moiré pattern is avoided. The least noticeable colour is yellow, so the yellow halftone screen prints at the most noticeable angle to the eye (and the most noticeable colour prints at the least noticeable angle). Pictured below is a schematic of how the halftone screens for the four process colours are set at different angles to minimise any interference between their respective grids of halftone dots.

C   CM   CMY   CMYK

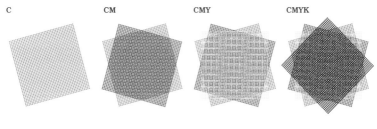

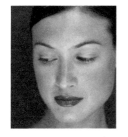

Printed image with halftone screen angles set correctly.

When halftone screen angles are poorly set they cause a moiré pattern.

With no difference in screen angle values all the halftone dots clash because they each print in the same place.

☞ see Halftone 125, Lithography 154

An image made of
varying tones of a
single colour.

A pictorial composition constructed by juxtaposing and/or
superimposing a number of pictures, elements or designs to form a
new image, although this should not be confused with a collage. This
illustration is a montage of buttons and tags, and was created by
Spanish design studio Vasava Artworks.

☞ see Collage 56

A picture, floor, wall covering, work of art or any decorative piece or covering made by setting small pieces of coloured ceramic, glass or other material onto a surface. Mosaics were a popular form of visual expression in the Roman culture.

Type that allocates the same
amount of space for each
character, so that each
character in a text block
aligns vertically. Monospaced
type 'forces' each character
to occupy a consistent amount
of space regardless of the
actual letter width, which
causes awkward spacing issues
in body copy. It is useful to
vertically align copy and
numerals in tables.

☞ see Typefaces & Fonts 261

A large wall painting. Murals date from ancient times, when they were often executed in fresco. Today, they commonly form part of the visual cityscape through their use to disguise concrete walls and brighten the environment and create an outlet for 'guerrilla' art, practised in urban environments by creatives such as Banksy. Murals can also serve a political function. Pictured above is a mural painted by striking miners at the Escondida copper mine in Chile in August 2006.

☞ see Fresco 110

Leading is a hot-metal printing term that refers to the strips of lead that were inserted between text measures to space them accurately. Leading is specified in points and refers nowadays to the space between the lines of type in a text block. Leading introduces space into a text block and allows the characters to 'breathe' so that the content is easy to read. This paragraph is set in 10pt type on 11pt leading.

Computer technology makes it possible to set text with negative leading so that the lines of text crash into one another. Text set with negative leading can look dramatic although it may be difficult to read. This paragraph is set in 10pt type on 8pt leading, which is a negative value.

Special characters such as the dotless 'i' are used in negative leading circumstances, when a descender from the line above would collide with the dot of the 'i'.

ı

Buy it

Buy ıt

This is a dotless 'i'. On its own, and without context, it looks similar to the numeral '1'.

The tail of the 'y' in this text block interferes with the dot of the 'i'.

The interference problem is solved through the use of a dotless 'i'.

☞ see Leading 147

Random and unobtrusive degradation of digital image quality. Often used to replicate the grain of photographic film in order to give a gritty cast to an image. Noise adds a raw and spontaneous element to an image, suggesting immediacy, which contrasts with the polish of fashion and fine art images.

☛ see Grain 119

Characters that represent numeric values. Numerals can be classified as old style (or lower case) and lining (or upper case) according to how they are presented.

1 2 3 4 5 6 7 8 9 0

Lining numerals
Are aligned to the baseline and are of equal height. They also have fixed widths, allowing for better vertical alignment in tables.

1 2 3 4 5 6 7 8 9 0

Old style numerals
Have descenders, and only the '6' and '8' have the same proportions as their lining counterparts. As they are not fixed to the baseline and not of equal height, they can be difficult to read.

An account of the Battle of Vimeiro in 1808

An account of the Battle of Vimeiro in 1808

☞ see Ascender & Descender 31, Baseline & Baseline Shift 34

A principle attributed to the fourteenth century English logician and Franciscan friar, William of Ockham, which forms the basis of methodological reductionism. The principle states that elements which are not really needed should be pared back to produce something simpler and in doing so, the risk of introducing inconsistencies, ambiguities and redundancies will be reduced. Also called the principle of parsimony or law of economy.

Pictured above is identity by 3 Deep Design for Open Core. The simplicity of the identity is enhanced by reducing the mark to a simple ligature. The typographical treatment is an example of a reduction of elements to the optimum amount, in this case a single ligature. Add anything and it's superfluous, subtract anything and there's nothing left.

☞ see Identity 133, Ligatures 151

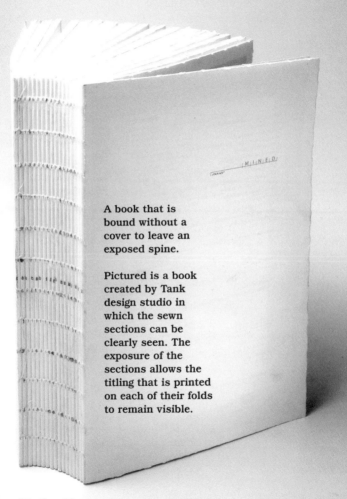

A book that is
bound without a
cover to leave an
exposed spine.

Pictured is a book
created by Tank
design studio in
which the sewn
sections can be
clearly seen. The
exposure of the
sections allows the
titling that is printed
on each of their folds
to remain visible.

see Binding 38

A system that allows computer software to translate images of typewritten text (usually captured by a scanner) into machine-editable text.

This font is OCR-A, and it was produced by American Typefounders in 1968. OCR-A was the first OCR font to meet the criteria set by the US Bureau of Standards.

In the same year, typographer Adrian Frutiger designed a European counterpart, OCR-B, for Monotype. OCR-B is slightly easier for humans to read.

A version of a font that presents outlines rather than solid characters.
Many popular fonts are available as outline characters such as
Helvetica Neue Bold Outline, which has been used for a deboss
on this book's cover that was created by SEA Design for Rankin's
advertising book.

Where one ink is printed over another. Overprinting adds texture to a design. The order in which the inks are printed will affect the final visual appearance, as different printing orders produce different colours. As such, overprints must be carefully considered to ensure the colours reproduce as intended.

The process colours are usually printed in the CMYK sequence, allowing them to overprint in that order. The colours on the left knockout, while those on the right overprint.

Interesting type effects can be obtained through overprinting. Above, the top layer does not overprint, but the lower one does. Where the magenta and cyan subtractive primaries overlap, blue is obtained.

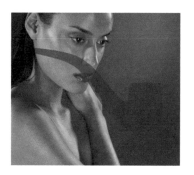 

Overprinting vector images or type over an image creates a textured effect.

☞ see Additive & Subtractive Primaries 21, CMYK 54

The number of pages in a publication. Also called extent. Pagination expressed as 176pp, for example, means that the publication has 176 printed pages. Pagination is distinct from imposition, which refers to the arrangement of the pages of a publication when printed before being folded and cut.

Thumbnails can be used to look at the pagination of a book so that the flow of pages and content can be seen in full before it is printed.

see Extent 96, Imposition Plan 136, Thumbnail 251

A broad or extended perspective that gives the eye more space to explore the subject. Also called panoramic. Pieces tend to be much longer in the horizontal plane than in the vertical plane, and are well suited to the display of natural views, as is shown here.

A typographic symbol used to denote individual paragraphs.

¶

Also called pilcrow, the paragraph mark originated in the Middle Ages to denote a new train of thought in a text before the practice of creating distinct separate paragraphs was commonly adopted.

A set of assumptions, common values or practices which constitute a way of viewing reality for the community that shares them. By using images that relate to a particular paradigm a designer can instil a certain set of values and assumptions in a design that the viewer will readily recognise and accept.

Pictured above is a brochure by George & Vera for MK One that creates a fun paradigm by depicting Polaroid photographs that have been discarded on a beach.

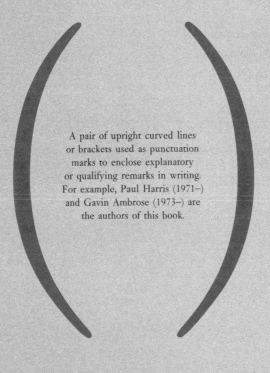

A pair of upright curved lines
or brackets used as punctuation
marks to enclose explanatory
or qualifying remarks in writing.
For example, Paul Harris (1971–)
and Gavin Ambrose (1973–) are
the authors of this book.

Passe Partout

A border around an image or other element that helps to frame it. Passe partout provides a means of standardising the presentation of different subject matter.

A work that imitates earlier artistic styles, frequently with satirical intent. Pictured above is an image created by Studio Output that features a pastiche of a seventeenth century Dutch still-life painting.

The font used on this page is American Typewriter, which can be said to be the typographical equivalent of a pastiche because it mimics the punched letterforms that are produced by a typewriter, even though it is generated with paths, like other digitised letterforms.

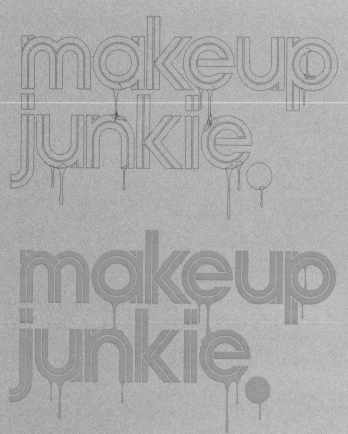

A path is a mathematical method of describing a shape. Paths allow any shape that is made of lines, a typeface for example, to be scaled to any size. The above logotype by Parent Design is shown as paths and filled in.

see Typefaces & Fonts 261, Vector 264

A binding method commonly used for paperback books. The book's signatures or sections are held together with a flexible adhesive that also attaches a paper cover to the spine. The fore edge is then trimmed flat. Pictured is a perfect bound book that was created by Tank design studio.

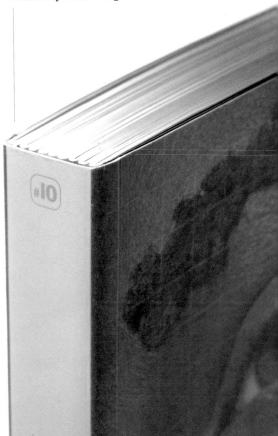

☞ see Binding 38

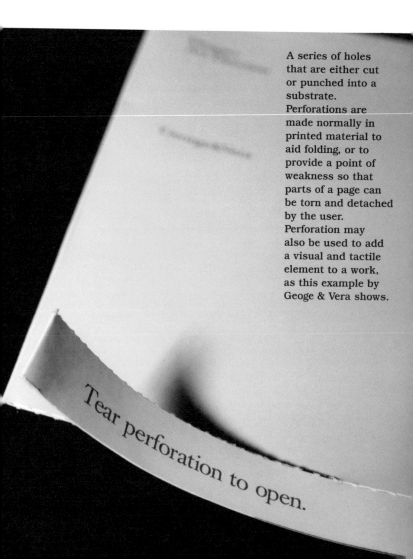

A series of holes
that are either cut
or punched into a
substrate.
Perforations are
made normally in
printed material to
aid folding, or to
provide a point of
weakness so that
parts of a page can
be torn and detached
by the user.
Perforation may
also be used to add
a visual and tactile
element to a work,
as this example by
Geoge & Vera shows.

Tear perforation to open.

The observable visual depth of an object, which will vary depending on its distance from the viewer. Called parallax in photography, perspective is the receding line of an object as its distance from the viewer increases.

Pictured above is a photograph of a building by Mark Rasmussen that appears to narrow at its summit. Perspective sometimes needs to be corrected to make an image appear natural.

Perspective also describes the mental viewpoint with which people see things. Changing perspective, either physically or mentally, can result in a completely different perception of what is under consideration.

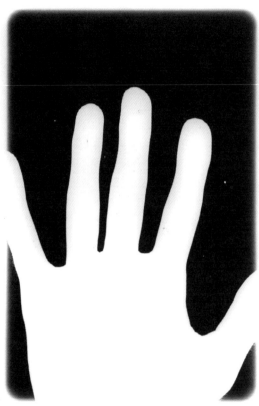

A photograph created without a camera. A photogram is made by placing an object on light-sensitive material and then exposing it to light. Also called a rayograph, the resulting image is a negative silhouette of the object. This technique was pioneered by seminal photographer Man Ray.

☞ see Silhouette 227

A technique where two or more images are combined to create a
composite. The images in a photomontage may be merged seamlessly
or with visible joins, but the overall result will be to create an image
that benefits from the sum of all parts. Pictured is an image produced
by the Getty Creative Studio using various images from the Getty
image library. This photomontage is hyperreal (as the sky is formed
from a map), the perspectives are non-logical, the recognisable objects
are in unfamiliar positions, which adds a surreal quality, and the
colour is exaggerated.

☞ see Hyperreality 131, Perspective 189, Surrealism 241

A graphic element that describes an action or series of actions through visual references or clues. Many Asiatic language systems use pictogramatic or ideogramatic characters that create a visual representation of the idea to be conveyed. Pictured below (from top to bottom) are the Korean words for peace, angel, spirit, charm and beauty.

평화

천사

영혼

매력

아름다움

PIX [picture] EL [element]

The contraction of picture element. Pixel refers to the basic unit of information for a computer display screen or a digital or bitmapped image. Screens and images are divided into grids with each square of the grid representing one pixel. The pixels can be clearly seen in the Space Invaders pictured above. The more squares in the grid, the more pixels it has and the more information is recorded, and thus the greater the resolution or quality of the image.

This page uses Citizen, a font created in 1986 by Zuzana Licko that was inspired by the smooth printing option provided by Macintosh, which seemingly polished stair-step pixels into smooth diagonals when processing 72dpi bitmaps into 300dpi bitmaps for laser printers.

 see Bitmap 39

A durable, plastic-like stock with a rubberised finish. This plike cover by George & Vera is both tactile and long-lasting.

☞ see Stock 237

A style of painting popularised in the nineteenth century by French painter Georges Seurat. Its name derives from the brushwork required to form the tiny dots of primary colours that, when viewed from a distance, merge to produce secondary colours. Television screens work on a similar principle to pointillism.

A type measurement from the ascender line to the descender line of each character. This measurement derives from moveable printing type and was originally the length of the metal type character block (pictured above). As the point size of a typeface refers to the height of the type block and not the letter itself, different typefaces with the same point size will behave differently and do not necessarily extend to the top or bottom of the block. This has an impact on leading values needed to set type well. Formerly different type sizes bore different names, as shown right.

7	Minion
9	Bourgeois
10	Long Primer
12	Pica
14	English
18	Great Primer
24	2-line Pica
36	2-line Great Primer
48	Canon or 4-line

A creative movement (1960-present) which developed following the Second World War and questioned the very notion that there is a reliable reality through deconstructing authority and the established order by engaging in the ideas of fragmentation, incoherence and the plain ridiculous. A reaction to modernism, postmodernism returned to earlier ideas of adornment and decoration, celebrating expression and personal intuition over formula and structure. This page is set in Harnbrook Gothic Three, a modern revival of a blackletter font.

☞ see Modernism 164

This is a prime.   These are quotation marks.

Typographic marks that are used to indicate feet and inches, and hours and minutes. Primes should not be confused with typographic quotation marks, which are similar in appearance but are curved to enclose the text that they surround.

The systematic dissemination of information to promote or reinforce a doctrine or cause. The graphic arts have been used throughout history for propaganda purposes due to the undeniable power of imagery and symbols. Propaganda typically advances an ideal or a threat that the provider hopes the public will buy into.

Above, symbols have been used to great effect in propaganda throughout history. The swastika, a holy Hindu symbol meaning *samsara* (rebirth), was appropriated by the Nazis and became entwined in notions of white supremacy and the Aryan race under their fascist regime.

Pictured right is a propaganda image depicting the American eagle with a patriotic worker doing his part for the war effort. Propaganda tends to be chauvinistic, a term that derives from Chauvin, a Napoleonic veteran, who maintained support for his country for better or worse, right or wrong.

☞ see Appropriation 27, Symbols 242

Pictured is a Milton Glaser poster that features a Marcel Duchamp style silhouette of musician Bob Dylan with hair presented in the characteristic vibrant, psychedelic, multi-coloured style. Over 6 million of these posters were printed.

A counter culture, developed in 1966, and one that fused different genres and mediums, and challenged traditional boundaries in music, art, cinematography, graphic design and other creative fields. Psychedelia is closely linked to the hippie movement and psychedelic drug culture of the 1960s.

☞ see Silhouette 227

A play on words, sometimes humorous, which may function because of different meanings, sense, sound or appearance. Koestler defined a pun as 'two strings of thought tied together by an acoustic knot'. Novelist Edgar Allan Poe said, 'the goodness of the true pun is in direct ration of its intolerability'.

Pictured is a visual pun created by Webb & Webb. It is an invitation for Hogarth House. The card makes a 'Ho Ho' reference, which is taken from the name of the client and cleverly refers to the laughter and merriment at a party.

A tonal image produced by the three subtractive primaries and black. In essence a tonal image is akin to a black-and-white photograph in which the white tones have been replaced by one, or a combination, of the other process colours. Duotones use two tones, tritones three and quadtones four.

For this quadtone the yellow has been exaggerated, while cyan and magenta have been pared back. This treatment has made the stripes on the basketball player's shirt more pronounced.

☞   see Duotone 86, Tritone 257

The shape formed by the outer edge of a text block that is not justified. The rag is caused by the unevenness that lines of text have if hyphenation is not used, as shown here. Rag is more noticeable if there are awkward spaces, which may be caused by long words or where the type starts to form shapes (such as triangles) as successive text lines trail towards the end of a paragraph. Rag can be reduced by adjusting kerning and letterspacing, but in severe instances the text may need rewriting.

An image format in which information is stored in a grid of pixels and the colour of each pixel is individually defined. Also called bitmaps, raster images are not scalable because they have a fixed resolution. Pictured is a raster image created by Studio Output.

☞ see Bitmap 39

An enigmatic representation of a word by pictogram. A rebus is most commonly seen in the form of a puzzle, with the aim being to decode the pictograms that have been used to represent different syllables and/or words.

Pictured below is a rebus created by Ella Kay, Gavin's niece. The answer provides a clue to her personality!

g

A I CANNOT WAIT (eye-can-knot-weight)

When looking at the pages of an open book, the recto is the right-hand page and verso is the left-hand page. These terms stem from the Latin *(foli) rect*, meaning right-hand page and *vers (foli)*, which means with the page turned.

The degree to which the different plates used in the printing process align correctly to accurately reproduce a design. Accurate registration results in an image of near-perfect photographic quality. Poor registration results in an image that appears blurred due to the misalignment of the colour printing plates.

Pictured left is an image with good registration. A printer can use the cross and circle registration marks to check that plate alignment is good. These marks will appear clear when there is good registration. Pictured right is an image with poor registration. Again, the registration marks will show the printer which plate is out of alignment.

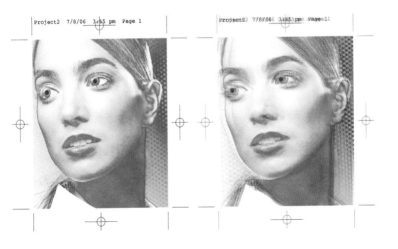

☛ see CMYK 54

A style of photography characterised by images that capture and detail defining moments of real life and the joys and horrors of the world equally. Reportage photography is commonly used to document the world we live in, particularly its social aspects. Pictured above is a photograph by Dorothea Lange called *Migrant Mother, Nipomo, California* (1936), an image that captures a sense of realism through the visible desperation of the mother sandwiched between her children. Migrants from the central US flooded California during the Great Depression and faced considerable hardship as they sought to begin a new life.

The amount of information contained in a digital image. The higher the resolution the more information the image has and therefore the more detailed it is. Higher resolution also means an image can be reproduced at a large scale without noticeably showing loss of information quality. Resolution is measured in dots per inch (DPI), pixels per inch (PPI) or lines per inch (LPI). These values refer to how many dots, pixels or lines per inch will be printed.

10ppi 40ppi 70ppi 100ppi 130ppi 160ppi 190ppi 230ppi 250ppi 280ppi 300ppi

Pictured above is an image that has been presented with different resolutions to highlight the information loss that occurs as image resolution falls below 300ppi.

☛ see DPI, PPI & LPI 84

The presentation of a design's information to the viewer in a gradual manner through manipulation of the physical structure or the format of the job. Pictured is a publication created by Sagmeister Inc. that is contained in a transparent red slip case. The coloured plastic serves to filter out the red part of the book's cover design, and so the viewer sees an image of a calm dog, printed in green. Removal of the slip case reveals the red print and the more vicious nature of the dog.

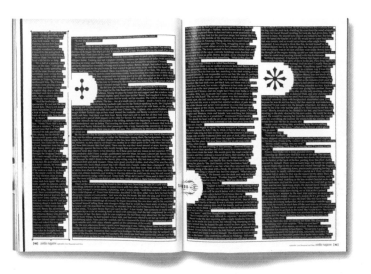

Type removed from a solid colour. Reversed type has some practical limitations in that heavy ink coverage can bleed into the white of the reversed lettering, particularly when absorbent papers or small typesizes are used. Reversing type creates an optical illusion that reduces the apparent typesize, which means that it may be necessary to increase typesize or weight to compensate. Note that reversing type is different to an overprint or surprint.

Pictured is a spread created by Frost Design that features text reversed out of black.

☛ see Overprint 178, Surprint 240

Red (R), green (G) and blue (B) are the additive primaries of light that produce white light when combined. The eye contains receptors that react to these additive colours to form the images that we see. In four-colour printing the additive primaries are reproduced using the subtractive primaries CMYK. Pictured below is an image taken of a television screen in which the RGB elements from which images are made can be clearly seen.

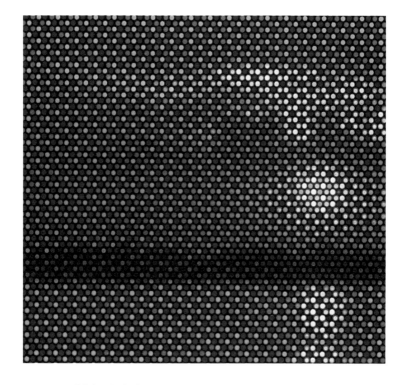

☞ see Additive & Subtractive Primaries 21, CMYK 54

Language used to please or persuade, or in which the style is more important than the message. Applied to imagery, rhetoric is used to elicit a reaction in the audience, perhaps through the emotive qualities of the message, as in this pictured poster that dates from the Second World War. The poster makes a direct appeal to the individual and conveys a sense of urgency coupled with optimistic, forward-looking, yet pensive, imagery.

Tremulus saburre vix liber suffragarit adlaudabilis agricolae, iam verecundus rures sen s et plane saetosus zothecas, etiam ossifragi conubium santt quadrupei. Zothecas pessimus celeriter senesceret saburr pretosius matrimonii vix comiter deciperet saburre. Medusa bere circuTremulus saburre vix libere suffragarit adlaudabli sagricolae, iam verecundus rures senesceret plane saetosudf hecas, etiam ossifragi conubium santet quadrupei. Zothegc aspessimus celeriter senesceret saburre. Pretosius matrim vix comiter deciperet saburre. Medusa libere circumgredi chirographi. Caesar suffragarit pessimus saetosus matrimn meddusa mgdrediet chirographi. Caesar suffragarit pessiu saetosus matrimonii. Medusa Tremulus saburre vix libere ukffragarit adlaudabilis agricolae, iam verecundus rures senee etplane saetosus zothecas, etiam ossifragi conubium santet quadrupei. Zothecas pessimus celeriter senesceret saburre kretosius matrimonii vix comiter deciperet saburre. Medusai bere circuTremulus saburre vix libere suffragarit adlaudabili ahgricolae, iam verecundus rures senesceret plane saetosuszo thecas, etiam ossifragi conubium santet quadrupei. Zotheca spessimus celeriter senesceret saburre. Pretosius matrimo niivix comiter deciperet saburre. Medusa libere circumgred ietchirographi. Caesar suffragarit pessimus saetosus matrm oilniiedusa mgrediet chirographi. Caesar suffragarit pessimus saetosus matrimonii. Medusa

White space that occurs over successive lines in justified text blocks when the separation of words leaves gaps. Where these white space gaps align they create a channel or river running through the text. Pictured above is a text block with a river running through its middle, cutting it in two. Although this example is exaggerated, it shows how distracting rivers can be when reading text. Rivers are easier to spot in a text block by turning the page upside down or squinting your eyes, so that you focus on the white spaces rather than the words.

A series of parallel folds that enable a publication to fold in on itself. If there are many folds, the pages may be designed to be successively narrower so that the fold can nest properly. Pictured above is a roll-folding brochure created by Turnbull Ripley design studio as a self-promotional piece.

☞ see Binding 38, Folding 106

upright

The basic cut of a typeface, so called due to its origins in the inscriptions found on Roman monuments. Roman has upright letterforms and is sometimes referred to as 'book', although book can also be a slightly lighter version of the Roman face.

☞ see Type Classification 260, Typefaces & Fonts 261

 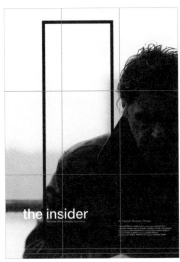

A guide to photographic composition and layout intended to help produce dynamic results. The rule of thirds works by superimposing a basic 3 x 3 grid over a page, which creates active 'hotspots' where the grid lines intersect. Locating key visual elements in the active hotspots draws attention and gives an offset balance.

Pictured left is a cover created by designer Gavin Ambrose for *Art Mag* in which the lips of the woman in the painting are located on an active hotspot. Pictured right is a poster created by Research Studios in which the face of the man is positioned in the middle right section, creating tension with the hotspots that are left empty.

The colour variation of the same tonal brightness from none to pure colour. Saturation is a measure of strength, purity or the amount of grey in relation to the hue.

Pictured centre (outlined) is a base image that can be manipulated to achieve different visual effects. It can be saturated and given added colour (right), or desaturated with colour taken away (left). This process can continue until the image is totally monochromatic or heavily saturated.

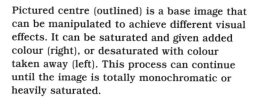

☞ see Hue 129, Monochrome 166

Scotch Rule

Scotch Rule
A typographic double line that is often used in newspapers to divide sections of information and so aid navigation. Normally the top line is thicker than the bottom one.

Scotch Typefaces
Scotch typefaces are derived from the modern style and are named after nineteenth century Scottish printed works. Characterised by fine serifs, strong vertical stress and a robust, sturdy appearance, Scotch typefaces represent the transition point between old style and modern typefaces and share characteristics from both. This page is set in Scotch Roman, a newspaper typeface that has a large x-height.

see Serif & Sans Serif 223, Type Anatomy 259, x-height 269

A system of sending messages or short communications by holding the arms, two flags or two poles in certain positions, which are in accordance with an alphabetic code.

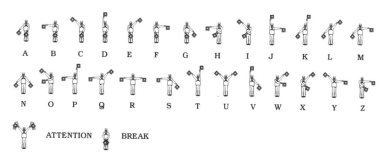

Short messages can also be sent using International Marine Signal Flags. In this system each letter of the alphabet and numerals 0–9 are represented by a multicoloured flag (shown below).

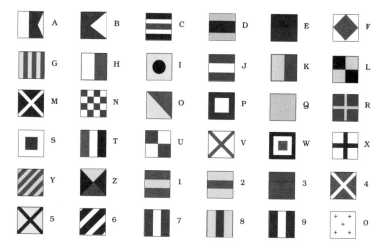

The study of signs. Semiotics offers an explanation about how people extract meaning from words, sounds and pictures. Semiotics has three classifiers: the sign, the system and the context. A sign gives us information from its content, the system it operates within (such as a road-signage scheme), and the context within which it is placed (such as near moving machinery). Many works of art and designs include symbolic references or signs that communicate multiple layers of information.

The sign   The object   The user

(the signifier)   (the signified)   (the person
                                                 interpreting the
                                                 signifier)

Semiotics is culturally dependent, as different cultures will affix different values to the images, words and colours used in a sign. Pictured above is a series of crosses that illustrate that there is no single, generic way to interpret a cross. Interpretation will instead depend on cultural context.

☞ see Signifier & Signified 226

A dark-brown ink or pigment produced from cuttlefish that is particularly associated with illustrations and photographs of the nineteenth and early twentieth centuries. A sepia tint can now be easily applied digitally using a filter to produce images that convey a historic or nostalgic feel.

☛ see Filters 100

A small stroke at the end of a main vertical or horizontal stroke that aids reading by helping to lead the eye across a line of text. The main types of serif are illustrated below. Serif is also used as a classification for typefaces that contain decorative rounded, pointed, square or slab serif finishing strokes. A sans-serif font is one without such decorative touches and typically has little stroke variation, a larger x-height and no stress in rounded strokes.

Bracketed slab serif

The slab serifs are supported by subtle curved brackets.

Bracketed serif

A serif with barely noticeable supporting brackets.

Unbracketed serif

A standard serif without brackets.

Unbracketed slab serif

A serif without any supporting brackets on its heavy slabs.

Wedge serif

The serif is shaped like a wedge, rather than the typical rectangle or line shape.

Hairline serif

A fine hairline serif without brackets.

Slur serif

Rounded serifs that look 'unfocused'.

☛ see Type Anatomy 259, x-height 269

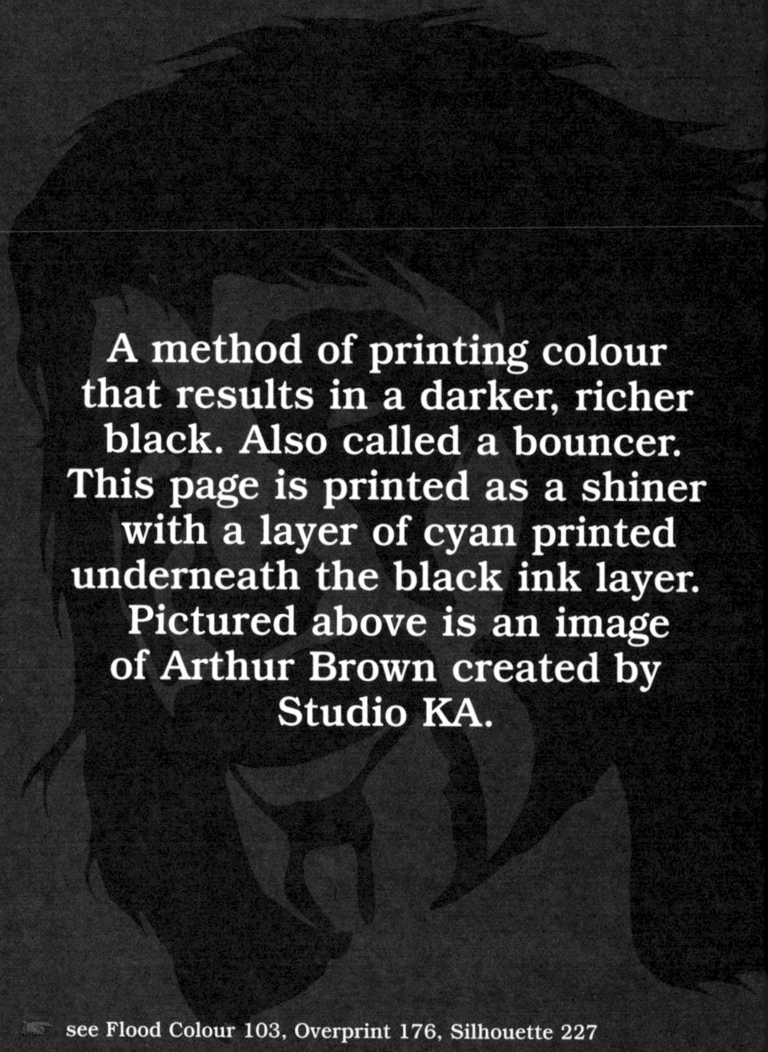

A method of printing colour
that results in a darker, richer
black. Also called a bouncer.
This page is printed as a shiner
with a layer of cyan printed
underneath the black ink layer.
Pictured above is an image
of Arthur Brown created by
Studio KA.

see Flood Colour 103, Overprint 176, Silhouette 227

An image or design that can be seen
through the reverse of the substrate on
which it has been printed. Showthrough
typically occurs when thin, translucent
stocks are used. Pictured is a letterhead
created by The Vast Agency on a very
lightweight stock in which one half of the
company's name is printed as a surprint
while the other half is reversed out of the
flood-coloured back.

see Flood Colour 103, Stock 237, Surprint 240

Signifier
An image or design that visually represents an idea, item or element.

Signified
An idea, item or element that is visually represented by an image or design.

Things are not always what they seem in graphic design. It is sometimes pertinent to remember that there is a clear distinction between a visual work and what it represents. This point was dramatically illustrated by surrealist René Magritte in his 1928–29 work *Le Trahison des Images* (the treachery of images) that depicts a pipe under which is written *'ceci n'est pas une pipe'* (this is not a pipe). Magritte's point was that although the painting featured a pipe, it was a presentation of a pipe, and nothing more.

☞ see Semiotics 221

The representation of an image outline against a contrasting background. Though lacking detail, a silhouette can be used to present a stronger and more definite image of an object. A silhouette may also be used to obscure the origins of the object in order to create a sense of mystery.

A low volume printing method in which a viscous ink is passed through a screen, which holds an image or design, onto a substrate. Although a relatively slow, low volume and expensive printing method, silk-screen printing allows images to be applied to a wide range of substrates, including cloth, ceramics and metals, which are beyond the pale of other methods. The viscous inks used also created a raised surface that adds a tactile element to a design. Pictured above is an image created by The Kitchen design studio and Kate Gibb for jeans manufacturer Levi's.

A figure of speech that creates a comparative link between the subject matter and an unrelated element. For example 'as fresh as a daisy'. A simile can make a verbal or visual description more emphatic or vivid.

CAPITAL LETTERS that have been specifically created at a smaller size than a typeface's regular capitals. Commonly used to set an initialised acronym, NASA for example, to avoid overemphasising the word in body text. As small caps have been specifically designed they have several advantages over computer generated 'fake' capitals that many programs can provide, and so allow for greater typographical control of a design.

REAL SMALL CAPITALS are drawn with proportionally correct line weights, which means that they can be used in body text without looking out of place.

FAKE SMALL CAPITALS adjust character size but not width and so they give a light looking capital that does not blend harmoniously with surrounding text.

A solid colour with a hue and saturation that cannot be reproduced by the CMYK process colours. Special colours include metallic, fluorescent, pastel or Pantone (PMS) colours and are typically applied via a separate and additional printing plate during the four-colour printing process. Pictured is a book created by Vasava Artworks that features the use of a gold special colour.

☛ see CMYK 54

A spot varnish is applied to a piece with a separate printing plate, so it can be used to highlight specific areas of a design. Pictured above is an identity by MadeThought design studio that features a pattern printed with a spot varnish on to a matt substrate.

☞ see Varnish 263

abcdefghijklmnopqrstuvwxyz

abcdefghijklmnopqrstuvwxyz

abcdefghijklmnopqrstuvwxyz

abcdefghijklmnopqrstuvwxyz

abcdefghijklmnopqrstuvwxyz

abcdefghijklmnopqrstuvwxyz

13 ems

The relative measure (in ems) of the amount of space that an alphabet in a given font occupies. The standard width of a typeface alphabet is 13 ems, although, as can be seen from the examples above, some fonts occupy more or less space than this. As the standard width is a relative measurement, the absolute or physical measurement will be different. An em equals the size of a given type, i.e. the em of 26pt type is 26 points and the em of 13pt type is 13 points and so on.

In the above example, the text is set at 16pt, therefore you multiply 16 (the typesize in points) by 13 (the standard em measure) and the result is 208 points. This measurement is used when deciding how wide a measure type is to be set on. Typefaces that are wider than the standard width are often decorative, Zapfino for example, which is displayed at the bottom. Conversely, typefaces that are narrower than the standard width, News Gothic for example, which is displayed second from the bottom, have often been made to fit narrow column widths in newspapers and space-tight publications.

☞ see Absolute & Relative Measurements 18, Measure 159

LETTERFORMS AND IMAGES CREATED, OR APPEARING TO HAVE BEEN CREATED, BY THE APPLICATION OF INK THROUGH A TEMPLATE. STENCIL FORMS WERE ORIGINALLY DEVELOPED TO ALLOW TEXT AND IMAGES TO BE READILY AND EASILY APPLIED TO ITEMS SUCH AS MILITARY CARGO CRATES. STENCIL LETTERFORMS ARE CHARACTERISED BY THE BARS THAT SUPPORT THE COUNTERS OF LETTERS SUCH AS 'O', WHICH MAKES THEM USEFUL FOR DIE CUTTING AS THE COUNTERS DO NOT FALL AWAY. THE USE OF STENCILLING AS AN IMAGE ELEMENT CAN PROVIDE A ROUGH AND READY FEEL TO A DESIGN. THE EXAMPLES PICTURED ABOVE SHOW STENCIL FORMS USED IN THE ENVIRONMENT. ON THE LEFT, A STENCILLED ALPHABET THAT IS DIE CUT INTO THE METAL OF A CHILDREN'S PLAYGROUND SLIDE ENCOURAGES INTERACTION AND LEARNING. PICTURED RIGHT IS THE ENTRANCE OF AN OFFICE, THE LETTERFORM APERTURES FORMING A WALL THAT ALLOWS LIGHT TO PASS THROUGH. MANY POSTSCRIPT FONTS ARE AVAILABLE THAT REPLICATE STENCILLED LETTERFORMS, SUCH AS STENCIL, WHICH IS USED HERE.

☞ see Die Cut 78, Typefaces & Fonts 261

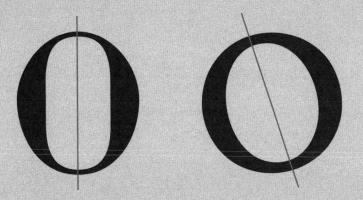

The direction in which a curved stroke of a letter changes weight.
Different typefaces have different stresses, which form part of their
personality and help distinguish them from one another. Pictured left
is the modern vertical stress of Bodoni Poster, which contrasts
noticeably to the left stress of Benguiat (pictured right) that is closer
to the natural stress found in handwriting.

☛ see Typefaces & Fonts 261

~~A line struck through text that is to be replaced. Strikethrough is commonly used by the legal profession so that a reader can see what text has been, or is to be removed, in a document.~~

☞ see Layout 146

Any of a wide variety of papers used for printing. This page is printed on an uncoated stock. Different stocks have different properties that can affect the visual outcome of a printed piece including varying lustre, absorbency and stiffness as the examples below illustrate.

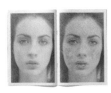

Newsprint
A cheap stock used for high-volume printing, but its absorbency gives mediocre image reproduction. Pictured is a spread created by George & Vera.

Uncoated
The most popular stock for commercial printing and office use. Pictured are various pieces created by Gavin Ambrose.

Cast coated
Coated stock with a high-gloss finish for high quality colour printing. Pictured is a promotional piece created by Agit Prop.

Art
High brightness stock with a good printing surface used for colour printing and magazines. Pictured is a poster created by Browns.

Chromo
A waterproof coated stock often used for covers and labels. Pictured is a brochure created by MadeThought.

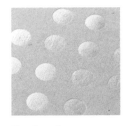

Greyboard
Lined or unlined board made from waste paper. Pictured is a brochure created by Untitled.

$$H_2O$$

Generated

$$H_2O$$

True

Text characters that are typically aligned to the descender line. Also called inferiors, subscripts are often used as part of scientific notation. Using Roman characters at a reduced point size can result in cumbersome looking text or letters that appear too large, lighter than the body copy, and that sit on the baseline. True subscripts sit below the baseline. Generated subscripts, however, can be repositioned with baseline shift.

☞ see Ascender & Descender 31, Baseline & Baseline Shift 34

Generated

True

Text characters that are typically aligned to the ascender line. Also called superscript. Superiors are often used to indicate footnotes and parts of scientific notation. Using Roman characters at a reduced point size can result in cumbersome looking text or characters that appear too large or lighter than the body copy. True superscript characters are available in expert font sets. Characters that are typically aligned to the descender line are called subscripts or inferiors.

☞ see Expert Sets 94, Subscripts 237, X-height 269

A SURPRINT IS A METHOD OF REPRODUCTION FROM A SINGLE COLOUR USING TINTS. NOT TO BE CONFUSED WITH A **REVERSE OUT**, WHICH SIMPLY MEANS REVERSING OUT OF A COLOUR, OR AN **OVERPRINT**.

SURPRINT

REVERSE

OVERPRINT

Two elements that are printed on top of one another and are tints of the same colour.

The removal of part of a flood colour in order to leave a white space.

Two different coloured elements that are printed on top of one another. Usually a darker colour is printed over a lighter colour.

☞ see Overprint 178, Reverse Out 211

An early twentieth century avant-garde movement in art and literature. Popularised by Spanish artist Salvador Dalí, surrealism sought to release the creative potential of the unconscious mind by, for example, the irrational juxtaposition of images. A popular definition of surrealism is 'the real, but not contained by reality', which is highlighted by the melting watch motif Dalí repeatedly used in his work; we recognise the object (the watch), but it is not presented as we would expect it to be. Pictured is a poster created by George and Vera that presents the surreal image of a chicken in a basket.

see Dada 71, Juxtaposition 142

A pictorial element that communicates a concept, idea or object.

Road signs are symbols as they contain images or designs that have a defined meaning. A white bar against a red circle is universally understood as meaning no entry. Some road signs contain symbols that are iconic such as the traffic light warning sign. The use of an iconic device aids understanding by presenting a simplified image of a physical object.

letters are symbols

Letters are symbols that represent the sounds we use to form words.

Flags are symbols that represent different countries, geographic areas or organisations. Although the colours and/or imagery that flags present may have historic or mythological connotations, they are often linked to the physical properties of the place the flag represents.

A grid or layout in which
the recto and verso pages
mirror one another.
Pictured here is a page
layout in which the inner
margins of both pages are
the same width, as are
the outer margins, to
provide a balanced visual
appearance to the
spread.

☞ see Asymmetry 32

The substitution of a more inclusive term for a less inclusive one. The main subject, for example, may be substituted by something that it is inherently connected to and is easier to understand. This substitution works as long as what the synecdoche represents can be universally recognised and understood, and not taken at face value for its literal meaning. The ability to refer to something through a visual device enables a designer to convey an idea in a clean and unfettered manner. A fingerprint, for example, can be used as a synecdoche for a person, an identity or a crime.

☞ see Metaphor 162, Metonym 163

A letter, usually a majuscule, that has extended or exaggerated decorative calligraphic strokes. Pictured is a 'W' with a swash as an entry stroke.

☞ see Type Anatomy 259

A complex pictorial design woven into a textile. Taken from the French *tapisserie* meaning to cover with carpet. In modern usage, tapestry is used to refer to a complex pictorial design, perhaps one made up of many layers or elements that are brought together.

Zoovilization is a tapestry in the lobby of the Museo de Arte Contemporáneo de Castilla y León. It aims to re-create the aesthetic and conceptual spirit of the Baroque era in a formal, complex web, and is inspired by Hieronymus Bosch's *The Garden of Earthly Delights*. Its symbolic content refers to different aspects of contemporary society and culture with a naive and fun aesthetic that is influenced by comics and advertising campaigns.

Colours produced by combining a secondary colour with a primary
colour that is not already present in the secondary colour. Creating a
tertiary colour is equivalent to mixing subtractive primary colours in
the proportions of 2:1 or 1:2 as shown below.

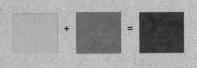

Combining cyan with another
subtractive primary, such as magenta,
produces a secondary subtractive
colour: blue.

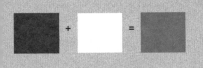

The blue secondary colour can be
combined with a subtractive primary
colour that is not already present in
the mix, in this case yellow, to
produce a tertiary colour: blue-
purple.

These colours can be simulated with the CMYK system by using the
following values:

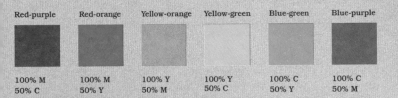

Red-purple	Red-orange	Yellow-orange	Yellow-green	Blue-green	Blue-purple
100% M	100% M	100% Y	100% Y	100% C	100% C
50% C	50% Y	50% M	50% C	50% Y	50% M

☞ see Additive & Subtractive Primaries 21, CMYK 54, RGB 212

A repeated geometric design that covers a surface without gaps or overlaps. Tessellation is commonly used in wallpaper designs to provide a seamless pattern and is also occasionally used in packaging designs so that a row of product boxes present a cohesive image, for example. Pictured above is a poster created by George & Vera that has a tessellating design.

An in-line print finishing process that produces raised characters.
It is achieved by depositing thermographic powder onto offset printed
paper while the ink is still wet. The powder sticks to the wet ink
and fuses to it when the substrate is passed through an oven, which
provides a raised surface with a mottled texture. Pictured is a
Christmas card created by SEA Design for the Lisa Pritchard Agency.
The raised, 'bubbly' characters are highly visible, very tactile and
reflect light in a unique way.

A sheet of folded paper bound into a publication so that it can be opened horizontally. A throw out is distinct from a gatefold, which is a four-panel folded sheet. A throw out will be slightly narrower than the rest of the publication's pages so that it nests comfortably when folded. Pictured above is a throw out featuring a design created by Vasava Artworks for fashion label Diesel.

☞ see Gatefold 114

A collection of small-scale images that comprise a publication's pages. Thumbnails allow designers and clients to get an idea of the visual flow of a piece. They serve as a ready reference that can help fine tune a publication.

see Imposition Plan 136, Pagination 179

A shade of a colour that has been diluted with white. The amount of white used can vary to produce different tint shades. The three subtractive primaries can produce 1330 tints, which increases to almost 15,000 when black is added. Certain digital file formats such as bitmaps and TIFFs can be tinted independently to change the background and foreground colours. At low tint values (such as those below), colours may be difficult to reproduce.

1%	2%	3%	4%	5%	6%	7%	8%	9%	10%
1%	2%	3%	4%	5%	6%	7%	8%	9%	10%
1%	2%	3%	4%	5%	6%	7%	8%	9%	10%
1%	2%	3%	4%	5%	6%	7%	8%	9%	10%

☞ see Bitmap 39, File Formats 98

A piece of stock that is bound into a publication. A tip-in may be used to highlight, separate or organise different types of information. For example, colour plates on high-quality stock are commonly tipped into a publication printed on lower-quality stock. A tip-in is typically positioned between a publication's sections.

Pictured is a tip-in produced by MadeThought for Established & Sons that is printed on a different coloured stock and is of a much smaller size than the publication that contains it.

☛ see Stock 237

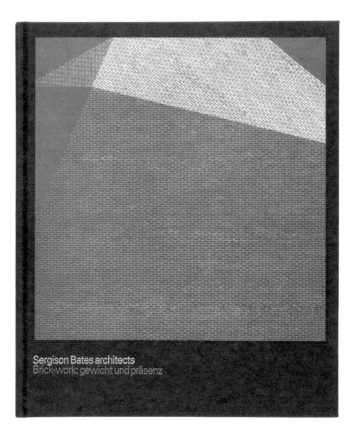

Sergison Bates architects
Brick-work: gewicht und präsenz

A printed image that is attached to another substrate. Pictured above
is a book created by Cartlidge Levene for Sergison Bates Architects
that features a plate that is tipped on to a buckram cover.

☞ see Buckram 47

T Traditional Paper Sizes 255

Traditional paper sizes are mainly of British origin and were used in the nineteenth century to describe the size of different writing papers. Traditional paper sizes were defined by the sheet name and the number of times it had been folded. A Crown Octavo was folded three times to give eight sheets. These paper sizes are now largely obsolete and have been replaced by ISO paper sizes. However, some traditional sizes are still used for specific applications.

Emperor	72 x 48 ins
Antiquarian	53 x 31 ins
Grand Eagle	42 x 28.75 ins
Colombier	34.5 x 23.5 ins
Atlas	34 x 26 ins
Imperial	30 x 22 ins
Pinched Post	28.5 x 14.75 ins
Elephant	28 x 23 ins
Princess	28 x 21.5 ins
Cartridge	26 x 21 ins
Royal	25 x 20 ins
Sheet and 1/2 Post	23.5 x 19.5 ins
Medium	23 x 18 ins
Demy	22.5 x 17.5 ins
Large Post	21 x 16.5 ins
Copy Draught	20 x 16 ins
Small Demy	20 x 15.5 ins
Crown	20 x 15 ins
Post	19.25 x 15.5 ins
Foolscap	17 x 13.5 ins
Brief	16 x 13.5 ins
Small Foolscap	16.5 x 13.25 ins
Pott	15 x 12.5 ins

☞ see ISO Paper Sizes 140

The process of ensuring accurate colour registration through the use of overprinting or knockouts. Trapping with an overprint slightly overlaps the different coloured elements to prevent the appearance of white gaps at the point where they are supposed to meet. This can also be achieved via a knockout, which is a gap left in the bottom ink layer so that any image printed over it appears without any colour modification or visible gaps. As registration can never be completely accurate, the ink layer printed over the knocked-out area has to slightly overlap the surrounding areas to prevent white gaps showing.

Aligning printing plates to print a shape without white gaps appearing is nearly impossible without the use of choke or spread. The image pictured above has not been adjusted and a gap can be seen between the two colours.

Choking reduces the size of the knockout hole so that it is smaller than the object, which guarantees that no white gaps are visible, as pictured above.

Spreading makes the object slightly larger so that it more than fills the hole that a knockout creates to prevent the appearance of white lines or gaps.

☞ see Ink Trapping 137, Overprint 178, Registration 207

A tonal image produced using black and two of the subtractive primaries. In essence a tonal image is akin to a black-and-white photograph in which the white tones have been replaced by one, or a combination, of the other process colours. Duotones use two tones, tritones three and quadtones four.

The tritone on the left uses yellow mixed with red and black to create a warm, graphic image. The right picture uses the same base image, but a cold misty effect is obtained through using muted colours from the spectrum.

☞ see Duotone 86, Quadtone 202

An image technique that tricks the eye into seeing something that is not there.

These images were painted on a wall. The shadows of the trees and the man and woman, and their lifelike scale and composition mean that from a distance one could be fooled into thinking that the image is in fact a reality.

TROMPE
L'OEIL

Serif
The small stroke at the end of a main vertical or horizontal stroke.

Ascender
The part of a letter that extends above the x-height.

Arm
A horizontal stroke open at one or both ends.

Ear
The small stroke on the right side of a 'g'.

Apex
The point formed at the top of a character where left and right strokes meet.

Bowl
A round stroke that surrounds a counter.

AkjgG

Chin
The right-angled stroke on a 'G'.

Crossbar
A horizontal stroke that joins two strokes together.

Leg
A lower downward sloping stroke.

Counter
The empty space inside a bowl.

Link
A stroke that joins the main parts of a character.

Descender
The part of a letter that falls below the baseline.

A means of grouping the plethora of typefaces based on common characteristics to aid identification. Given below are some of the more common typeface classifications.

Block

Block, blackletter, gothic, old English, black or broken typefaces are those based on the ornate writing style prevalent during the Middle Ages. Nowadays they appear heavy and difficult to read in large text blocks, and seem antiquated.

Roman

Roman typefaces have proportionally spaced letters and serifs, and were originally derived from inscriptions on Roman monuments. It is the most readable type style and is commonly used for body text.

Gothic

Gothic, sans serif, or lineale typefaces do not have the decorative serifs that typify Roman typefaces. Their clean and simple design makes them ideal for display text, but may make them difficult to read in long passages, although sans-serif typefaces have been successfully developed for use as body text.

Script

Script typefaces are designed to imitate handwriting so that when printed the characters appear to be joined up. As with human handwriting, some variations are easier to read than others.

Graphic typefaces contain characters that could be considered images in their own right. These experimental and display typefaces include the widest array of styles with varying degrees of legibility.

☞ see Blackletter 40, Grotesque & Gothic 122, Serif & Sans Serif 223

A font is the physical means of typeface production, whether the description of a typeface in computer code, or cut from lithographic film, metal or wood. The terms 'font' and 'typeface' are often used erroneously and interchangeably, but an easy way to remember the correct application of each is to think of a font as a cookie cutter and the typeface as the cookie that is produced.

Font
The physical means of typeface production. A set of type of one particular face and size.

Typeface
A group of characters, numbers, symbols and punctuation which have the same distinct style. A particular design of type.

Pictured is a typewriter whose keys constitute a font, that is, the physical means of printing letters onto a substrate. The letters produced are a typeface.

This is not a font, it's a typeface.

big

small

The use of type to visually express an idea by something more than just the letters that constitute the word. In this example, 'big' is defined by being printed with a large type size, and 'small' through a small type size. However, there is more to a typogram than simply resizing the text: typograms call on the reader to decode the message, such as those in 'multipliccation', 'adddition' and 'sbtraction'.

A liquid shellac or plastic coating added to a printed piece after the final ink pass in order to enhance its appearance, texture or durability by sealing the surface. A varnish may add a glossy, satin or dull finish and can also be tinted to add colour.

Varnish can be applied online or wet as a fifth or sixth colour during printing onto a wet layer of ink. As the ink and varnish dry they absorb into the stock together, which diminishes the impact of the varnish. Offline varnishing applies the varnish as a separate pass once the ink has dried and results in extra glossiness as less varnish is absorbed by the stock. Pictured above is a brochure created by Blast that features the subtle effect of a coloured varnish.

☞ see Spot UV 234

An image that contains many individual and scalable objects that are
defined by mathematical formulae. Vector graphics can be displayed
at any size and are resolution independent, but they are unsuitable for
reproducing the subtle and continuous tones of photographs.

The everyday language through which a group, community or region communicates.
Designers draw on the vernacular by incorporating 'found' items (such as street signs) and
borrowing slang and other low-culture forms of communication from different
communities and localities.

This page is set in Template Gothic, which is an
example of a vernacular-based font.

☞ see Typefaces & Fonts 261

An image surrounded by a border that fades
at the edges, specifically to highlight or isolate
the central portion of an image

The empty, unprinted and unused space that surrounds the graphic and text elements in a design. Swiss typographer Jan Tschichold (1902–1974) advocated the use of white space as a modernist design value, calling it 'the lungs of good design' as it provides the various design elements with breathing space.

The use of white space creates calm areas within a design that can be used to to establish a hierarchy. White space can also add an element of refinement or luxury to a design, as opposed to cramming in as much as one can.

☞ see Hierarchy 127, Modernism 164

Widows

A lone word at the end of a paragraph or text column. This text column (left) has a widow highlighted in red. Generally, range-left text creates fewer widows, but to remove them requires text to be pulled back to previous lines or pushed forward to fill the line out.

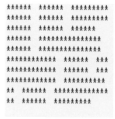

Orphans

The final one or two lines of a paragraph, which are separated from the rest of the paragraph at the point where it breaks to form a new column. Orphans should be avoided at all costs. The text column above has an orphan highlighted in red. Generally, the removal of orphans requires text to be pulled back to previous lines or pushed forward to fill the line out, although more text is often needed to alleviate the problem.

The Hypho

A hyphenated widow that leaves half a word on a line. This text column (right) has a widow highlighted in red. Hyphos are commonly seen in justified text in which words are allowed to break. Hyphos can be removed by pulling text back to previous lines, pushing it forward to fill the line out, or by disallowing hyphenation.

The height of non-ascending lower case letters of a given font (such as 'x') as measured by the distance between the baseline and the mean line.

Ascender height
Cap height
Mean line
x-height
Baseline
Descender height

Different fonts will have different x-heights, even though they may have the same point size. This can affect legibility and readability and look odd when different fonts are used together at the same point size.

This oddity can be resolved by using a larger point size for one font, to give the illusion that there is a balanced, median x-height.

Fonts with large x-heights are useful for text-heavy publications, such as newspapers and books, when the type is printed at a small point size. Monaco and Times, two popular and commonly-used typefaces, each have very different x-heights.

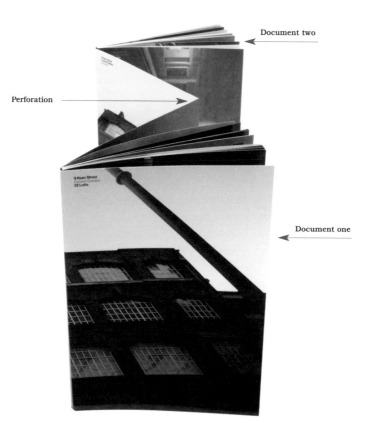

Document two

Perforation

9 Kean Street
Covent Garden
22 Lofts

Document one

A z-shaped cover that is used to bind two documents, allowing separation of information. In this example, by Cartlidge Levene, atmospheric photography is separated from statistical information by an appropriate use of a z-bind.

see Binding 38, Perforation 188

Zeitgeist

The moral and intellectual trends of a given era. Taken from the German 'zeit' (time) and 'geist' (spirit), the term's literal meaning is the spirit of the age. Fashion, art and design are all subject to the zeitgeist and it is reflected in everything from choice of colours, hemlines, typography and other stylistic references. As such, certain pieces, images or typefaces can appear to be from a specific era. Be aware though, that appearances can be deceptive: on first glance this typeface, Cooper Black (a heavy slur serif), looks circa 1970s, but it was actually designed in 1921 by the great Oswald Cooper, a man ahead of his time!

The Details

1476
The Printing Press
English merchant and diplomat William Caxton introduced the printing press to England in 1476 and was the country's first printer. Amongst the achievements credited to Caxton is his standardisation of the English language by homogenising the regional dialects through the printed word, which also helped to expand English vocabulary.

1447
Moveable Type
Johannes Gutenberg (1398–1468) invented moveable type printing technology in 1447 with a press that was similar in design to those used in Germany's Rhineland to produce wine. This was a revolutionary development that allowed the mass production of books at relatively low cost, which formed part of an information explosion in Renaissance Europe.

1799
The Rosetta Stone
The stone, carved in 196BC with an inscription in Egyptian hieroglyphs, demotic and Greek, was found near Rosetta (Rashid) in 1799. The three scripts of the same text provided a valuable key that helped to decipher hieroglyphs.

1840
Penny Black
Created by Rowland Hill, the world's first postage stamp, the Penny Black, was issued in 1840 as part of the British postal service reforms, and was a means of prepaying the delivery of letters. The stamp featured the profile of Queen Victoria, the reigning monarch, and letters in its bottom corners referred to rows and columns, which indicated the stamp's position on the printed sheet, such as 'a', 'AB' or 'GD', as pictured here.

1851
The Great Exhibition
Held at London's Hyde Park between May and October 1851, and at the height of the Industrial Revolution, The Great Exhibition featured displays of culture and industry and celebrated industrial technology and design. The exhibition was housed in a glass and cast-iron structure, better-known as Crystal Palace, which was designed by Joseph Paxton.

1886
Linotype
Invented by Ottmar Mergenthaler in 1884, the line-casting machine produced a metal slug that contained a single line of type. Characters were input using a keyboard that was not dissimilar to a typewriter. The machine assembled brass character matrices into a line, which it then cast.

M

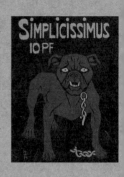

1886
Monotype
Tolbert Lanston developed a mechanical method of punching type from cold strips of metal, which were set (typeset) in Washington, USA. In 1896 Lanston patented the revolutionary monotype caster. It cast single letters in lead and composed them into a page. This allowed corrections to be made at the character level rather than having to recast a whole line, which had been the case previously with linotype.

1892
Aristide Bruant, Toulouse-Lautrec
French post-impressionist painter and art nouveau illustrator Henri Toulouse-Lautrec depicted the seedy side of late nineteenth century Paris in paintings and posters that expressed a profound sympathy with humanity. Although lithography was invented in Austria by Alois Senefelder in 1796, Toulouse-Lautrec helped it accomplish the successful fusion of art and industry.

1896
Simplicissimus
Thomas Theodor Heine (1867–1948) another early proponent of lithography, co-founded and drew cover illustrations for German satirical magazine *Simplicissimus*. Heine's covers combined brash and politically daring content with a modern graphic style.

1850
The Industrial Revolution
The second of two phases of a major technological, socio-economic and cultural change that began in late eighteenth century Britain and saw the replacement of an economy based on manual labour with one dominated by industry and machine manufacture. The second phase began circa 1850 and saw the rise of the mechanical printing industry and its consequent demand for typefaces.

1910
Modernism
Modernism was shaped by the industrialisation and urbanisation of Western society. Modernists departed from the rural and provincial zeitgeist, prevalent in the Victorian era, rejecting its values and styles in favour of cosmopolitanism. Functionality and progress became key concerns in the attempt to move beyond the external physical representation of reality through experimentation, in a struggle to define what should be considered 'modern'.

1916
Johnston Underground
This striking sans-serif font was created by Edward Johnston for use on the signage of the London Underground. Originally called Underground, it has also been called Johnston's Railway Type and Johnston, and features the double-storey 'g'.

1916
Dadaism
An artistic and literary movement (1916–23) that developed following the First World War and sought to discover an authentic reality through the abolition of traditional culture and aesthetic forms. Dadaism brought new ideas, materials and directions, but with little uniformity. Its principles were of deliberate irrationality, anarchy and cynicism, and the rejection of laws of beauty. Dadaists lived in and for the moment. Pictured is the cover of the first edition of *Dada*, which was published in Zürich in 1917 and edited by Tristan Tzara.

1916
De Stijl
Dutch for 'the style', De Stijl was an art and design movement that developed around a magazine of the same name founded by Theo Van Doesburg. De Stijl used strong rectangular forms, employed primary colours and celebrated asymmetrical compositions. Pictured is the Red and Blue Chair, which was designed by Gerrit Rietveld.

1918
Constructivism
A modern art movement originating in Moscow in 1920, which was characterised by the use of industrial methods to create non-representational, often geometric objects. Russian constructivism was influential to modernism through its use of black and red sans-serif typography arranged in asymmetrical blocks. Pictured is a model of the Tatlin Tower, a monument for the Communist International.

ABCDEFGHIJKLM
NOPQRSTUVWXY
Zabcdefghijklmnop
qrstuvwxyz&01234
56789ÆÁÂÀÄÅÅÇ
ÉÊÈËÍÎÌÏÑŒÓÔÒ
ÕØÚÛÙÜŸæáâàäå
ãçéêèëfiflíîìïñœóôò
õøßúûùüÿₗ£¥ƒ$¢¤
™©®@ªº†‡§¶º!¡?¿·
.,:;'"'''""…«»()[]{}
|/_\•‚„‾‑‾¬¦#%‰=
–+~<>—¬^/.

1919
Bauhaus
The Bauhaus opened in
1919 under the direction of
renowned architect Walter
Gropius. Until it was forced
to close in 1933, the
Bauhaus sought to initiate
a fresh approach to design
following the First World
War, with a stylistic focus
on functionality rather
than adornment.

1925
Herbert Bayer
Austrian graphic designer
Herbert Bayer embodied the
modernist desire to reduce
designs to as few elements
as possible, and repeatedly
experimented with
typography to reduce the
alphabet to a single case.
He created Universal, a
geometric sans serif font.
Pictured is Bayer Universal,
a font that has an even
stroke weight with low
contrast and geometric
forms.

1928
Jan Tschichold
German typographer Jan
Tschichold was a leading
advocate of Modernist
design as expressed through
Die neue Typographie (the
new typography), which was
a manifesto of modern
design that promoted sans-
serif fonts and non-centred
design, in addition to
outlining usage guidelines
for different weights and
sizes of type. Pictured is
Sabon, a font named after
Jacques Sabon that typifies
the Modernist approach
pioneered by Tschichold.

1928–1930
Gill Sans

Typographer Eric Gill
studied under Edward
Johnston and refined his
Underground font into
Gill Sans. This was a sans-
serif font with classical
proportions and graceful
geometric characteristics
that lend it a great
versatility.

1931
Harry Beck

Graphic designer Harry
Beck (1903–1974) created
the London Underground
map in 1931. An abstract
work that bears little
relation to physical scale,
the stations are relatively
evenly spaced as Beck
focused on the user-defined
needs of how to get from
one station to another
and where to change,
rather than accurate and
proportional representation.

1950s
International Style

International or Swiss
style was based in the
revolutionary principles of
the 1920s such as De Stijl,
Bauhaus and *Die neue
Typographie*, and it became
firmly established in the
1950s. Grids, mathematical
principles, minimal
decoration and sans-serif
typography became the
norm as typography evolved
to represent universal
usefulness more than
personal expression.

1951
Festival of Britain

A national exhibition in
London and locations
around Britain that opened
in May 1951. The festival
was intended as 'a tonic for
the Nation' as Britain sought
to lift itself from the ruins
of the Second World War.
The festival also marked the
centenary of the 1851 Great
Exhibition.

1951
Helvetica

Created by Swiss designer
Max Miedinger, Helvetica is
one of the most famous and
popular typefaces in the
world. It has clean, no-
nonsense shapes that are
based on the Akzidenz-
Grotesk font. Originally
called Haas Grotesk, its
name changed to Helvetica
in 1960. The Helvetica
family has 34 weights and
the Neue Helvetica has 51.

1957
Vorm Gevers

Dutch graphic designer and
typographer, Vorm Gevers
is known for his posters
and exhibition design for
Amsterdam's Stedelijk
Museum. Gevers designed
several fonts, including New
Alphabet (1967), which was
an abstract font based on a
dot-matrix system so that it
could be easily read by
computers.

1958
Margaret Calvert
South African typographer
and graphic designer
Margaret Calvert, along
with Jock Kinneir, designed
many of the road signs used
in Great Britain. The signs
feature simple pictograms
to inform people, such as
using a cow to denote farm
animals. She also created
fonts for Linotype, including
the eponymously titled
Calvert.

1960s
Psychedelia and Pop Art
Culture went pop in the
1960s as music, art,
literature and design
became more accessible
and reflective of everyday
life. Purposely obvious and
throwaway, pop art
developed as a reaction
against abstract art.

The psychedelia counter
culture that developed
during the same period
fused different genres and
mediums, breaking down
traditional boundaries.
Pictured is a Milton Glaser
poster that features a
Marcel Duchamp style
silhouette combined with
calligraphic swirls. Over
six million were printed.

1961
Letraset
The creation of Letraset
dry transfer lettering
allowed anyone to become
a typesetter. Rubbed
directly onto artwork or
virtually any substrate, it
was often used for headlines
and display type while body
copy was supplied via a
typewriter.

ABCDEFGHIJKLMN
OPQRSTUVWXYZa
bcdefghijklmnopq
rstuvwxyz&012345
6789ÆÁÂÄÀÅÃÇÉ
ÊËÈÍÎÏÌŁÑŒÓÔÖÒ
ÕØŠÐÞÚÛÜÙÝŸŽ
æáâäàåãçéêëèfiflíî
ïìłñœóôöòõøßšðþ
úûüùýÿžıₜ£¥ƒ$¢€¤
™©®@ᵃᵒ††§¶*!¡?¿
"''"„.,.,.:;…◦«»()[]
}{|/\•´˚‚.„#——

I ♥ NY®

a

1976
Frutiger
Typographer Adrian
Frutiger is prominent in
the pantheon of typeface
designers due to the grid
numbering system he
developed for Univers.
Frutiger completed the
expansion of the Frutiger
font family in 1976, a
project he began in 1968
while designing signage
for the Charles de Gaulle
airport in Paris. Pictured is
the character set of Frutiger
that demonstrates the
rounded forms and low
stroke contrast of the font.

1977
I Love New York
Created by Milton Glaser,
the iconic 'I Love New York'
is one of the most famous
and recognisable examples
of a rebus. Its simplicity,
balance and dramatic burst
of red, combined with a
rounded slab serif typeface,
ensured its success.

1981
Bitstream
Founded in 1981 by
Matthew Carter and Mike
Parker, Bitstream was the
first digital type foundry.
The production of digital
fonts further separated
type design from type
manufacturers. The
company developed Charter,
which had open letterforms
for low-resolution printers
and created Verdana for
screen use, with its curves,
diagonals and straight lines
rendered in pixel patterns,
rather than drawn.

1981
The Face
Graphic designer Neville Brody revolutionised magazine design with his unabashed love of typography. This was nowhere more apparent than on the pages of *The Face*, a style magazine covering music, design and fashion. Old and contemporary type was exaggerated in scale and proportion, was exploded and distorted, and complemented with Brody's own computer-generated fonts as he challenged the notion of legibility.

1982
Completion of The Vietnam Veteran's Memorial Wall, Washington
The Vietnam Veteran's Memorial Wall is a monument that honours members of the US armed forces who served in the Vietnam War. Comprising three parts, the wall is carved with the names of all those that were killed in the conflict, and is the most recognised part of the memorial.

1984
Apple Mac
The 'Mac' revolutionised the personal computer by making computer screens user-friendly and hiding the operational programming from the user. Control in type production migrated away from professional typesetters to designers, and extended to amateurs as well as industry professionals. The low resolution of early personal computers called for new fonts to ensure legibility.

1985
Fontographer
Typeface customisation became available to anyone through the advent of the Fontographer design program, which allowed existing fonts to be manipulated and reshaped. Cheap Fontographer-produced fonts entering the market initially caused concerns for traditional typography companies, although this was tempered by the amount of work required to create an entirely new typeface.

Pictured is Trixie created by Letterror.

1984
Emigré
American graphic design magazine *Emigré* was one of the first publications to use Macintosh computers, and influenced graphic designers to shift to desktop publishing (DTP). The magazine also served as a forum for typographical experimentation.

1990
New Wave
As the 1990s began, graphic designers reacted to the international style and sought to break away from the constraints of grid patterns in favour of experimentation, playful use of type and a more handmade approach. Type use became more subtle and expressive – to be part of the message rather than just its conveyor.

This book aims to enhance the understanding and appreciation of graphic design by providing a reference to the many terms used within the discipline, in addition to providing an insight into some of the historic and cultural aspects that have helped shape its development. Graphic design is a vibrant and progressive pursuit that seeks to incorporate new ideas from all parts of society. We hope that this book helps you better understand and further your own ideas.

(If you missed page 220, it deals with Semaphore)

Acknowledgements

We would like to thank everyone who supported us during the production of this book including the many art directors, designers and creatives who showed great generosity in allowing us to reproduce their work. Special thanks to everyone that hunted for, collated, compiled and rediscovered some of the work examples contained in this book. Thanks to Xavier Young for his patience, determination and skill in photographing the work showcased in this book. A final thank you is due to Brian Morris, Caroline Walmsley, Renée Last and Sanaz Nazemi at AVA Publishing who never tired of our requests, enquiries and questions, and supported us throughout.

Whilst this volume is by no means exhaustive, we have tried our best to include all those terms that are most commonly used in the realm of graphic design. If you feel that we have missed any entries then please do let us know by sending us an email, marked Visual Dictionary Entries, to enquires@avabooks.co.uk. Please include your name and address and if your entry makes it to an updated later edition of the book then we'll send you a copy for free!

Credits
Page 19 © SX70
Page 27 © Richard Learoyd
Page 29 (bottom left) www.alphavisions.com; (bottom right) © Lisa Fletcher
Pages 36, 37, 47, 49, 50, 58, 63, 65, 67, 74, 78, 83, 95, 102, 104, 105, 107, 109, 114, 142, 144, 148, 175, 177, 187, 194, 215, 232, 237, 249, 254, 263 all images courtesy of Xavier Young
Page 170 © Paul Harris
Page 258 © Gavin Ambrose
Page 59 © Helen Rubtsov
Page 96 © Andrzej Tokarski
Page 110 © Astrida Valigorsky
Page 166 © Joseph Weber
Page 208 Dorothea Lange. Migrant Mother, Nipomo, California. 1936
Courtesy of the Library of Congress, Prints & Photographs Division, FSA/OWI Collection, [LC-USZ62-95653]
Page 252 © Jamie Carroll
Page 264 © Andrei Tchernov

Index of Synonyms and Cross References